C OWLEY PUBLICATIONS is a ministry of the brothers of the Society of Saint John the Evangelist, a monastic order in the Episcopal Church. Our mission is to provide books and resources for those seeking spiritual and theological formation. Cowley Publications is committed to developing a new generation of writers and teachers who will encourage people to think and pray in new ways about spirituality, reconciliation, and the future.

LIVING WORDS

The Ten Commandments for the Twenty-first Century

G. Corwin Stoppel

Cowley Publications
Cambridge, Massachusetts

Library of Congress Cataloging-in-Publication Data:

Stoppel, Gerald C., 1952-
  Living words : the Ten Commandments for the twenty-first century /
  G. Corwin Stoppel.
    p. cm.
  Includes bibliographical references and index.
  ISBN 1-56101-271-8 (pbk. : alk. paper) 1. Ten Commandments—
Criticism, interpretation, etc. I. Title.
  BV4655.S76 2005
  241.5'2–dc22
                                2004026865

Cover design: Brad Norr Design

This book was printed in the United States of America on acid-free
paper.

Cowley Publications
4 Brattle Street
Cambridge, Massachusetts 02138
800-225-1534 · www.cowley.org

In memory of my father, Fabian, and in honor of my mother, Eleanore, who by word and example taught and lived out these commandments.

TABLE OF CONTENTS

✦

INTRODUCTION											1

CHAPTER ONE											5
Choosing the One over the Many

CHAPTER TWO											25
Embracing a Complex God

CHAPTER THREE										37
So Help Me, God

CHAPTER FOUR											51
Weekly Refreshment for Body and Soul

CHAPTER FIVE											65
Beyond Flowers and Power Tools

CHAPTER SIX											79
Taking Stock of Taking Life

CHAPTER SEVEN										99
From Harmony to Havoc

CHAPTER EIGHT										111
Nickel and Diming: Stealing Our Peace

CHAPTER NINE											119
Honest to God

CHAPTER TEN											129
A Peaceful Heart

EPILOGUE											139
Keeping It Simple: The Two Great Commandments

FOR CENTURIES MEN AND WOMEN have scrupulously studied and debated almost every aspect of the Ten Commandments. There have been scholarly debates on whether they were given to Moses by the Lord God precisely as we have them, or whether Moses slipped away for a time to write them on his own. There have been arguments about the similarities with other legal codes of approximately the same era or earlier. There have been constant arguments, by laypeople and theologians; by Christians, Jews, and Muslims; by people who have no belief in God; and by almost everyone else, as to what these commandments mean. There have been even more arguments about how they are to be applied in daily living, and whether they are even relevant in what we have come to call the post-Christian and postmodern world. In the summer of 2003, they became the object of considerable political and religious debate in Alabama when a state supreme court judge defiantly kept them on display in a public building. He claimed that the Ten Commandments were the basis for all our civil and criminal law. Many agreed with him. But others said that because of the constitutional separation of Church and state in the United States, one religion's code of behavior could not be given precedence over another's in a state building in this manner.

Those who have attempted to apply the commandments in their daily lives have soon discovered that they are almost impossible to fully obey. Though at first blush they appear simple, understanding them is a complex matter, because each generation examines them in light of their own culture, technology, and world.

For example, the sixth commandment states that we must not commit murder. But this was written at a time when abandoning deformed or retarded children on a mountainside was an acceptable practice, as was human sacrifice among some cultures. It was long before an era of abortion and euthanasia as we know them and more openly discuss them today, a time when genocide was an accepted fact between warring nations. The next commandment, the prohibition against adultery, is from an era when no one imagined such things as print or Internet pornography, some of the more risqué forms of public entertainment, and modern birth control devices.

It is little wonder that many people treat the commandments with awe and reverence while others dismiss or ignore them. Still others attempt to apply them, but find the task so overwhelming that they soon give up; yet others dedicate their entire lives to attempting to fulfill every implication arising from them. And then there are those who manipulate the spirit of the law, thinking, for example, that if they do not actually take the life of another person with premeditation, they have not violated the injunction against committing murder. Some people see them as confining—spoiling and limiting their pleasure and enjoyment in life—and others see them as the great parameters of personal and corporate social behavior, while still others hear them as words of incredible liberation and freedom.

2

In this swirling vortex of meaning, Christians are enjoined to understand them through Jesus' words and example. When asked about the commandments, Jesus said that if we so much as think and dwell on something that is forbidden by the Law, we are already as guilty as if we had performed the deed itself. What a formidable task we face!

As we look at the Ten Commandments as a whole, then, we can make several broad statements. First, despite the apparent simplicity of these laws, they are almost impossible to completely fulfill, not least because as Jesus, St. Paul, and countless others have commented, perfect obedience and perfection are beyond our capability. Thus, the commandments become our goal, the framework for personal and corporate relationships. In daily striving for this goal, we find ourselves living in greater harmony with the rest of the world and with God.

Second, the commandments give us a glimpse of what is possible when we live in harmony with God's best hopes for the world and each other rather than accepting the messy, confused, violent chaos that easily prevails. Glimpsing the perfection that we will find in heaven inspires us to take responsibility for keeping these commandments to create God's reign already on earth. From our growing realization of the universal sovereignty of God and his creation comes our passion for preserving the environment, protecting the rights of minorities and the disenfranchised, and establishing schools, hospitals, nursing homes, and other institutions that benefit all people. These laws are the basis for much of our civil and criminal law in the United States, and for our personal and public morality. No legal code can mandate and no judge can force an individual to honor his or her mother and father or to not be jealous of another's possessions. Rather, an individual chooses such goals to form their pattern for living.

Finally, because the commandments appear to be so simple and yet are so challenging to apply, we see more clearly the necessity of living an intentional life. So we choose to be fully engaged with them in our living—heart, body, and mind working together. Through the commandments we reach for an integrated life in which our words and actions are congruent, we come to know ourselves more fully, we better discern what God wants for us and from us, and then we opt to do it.

3

✦

Choosing the One over the Many

THE FIRST COMMANDMENT

*I am the Lord your God; you shall have
no other gods but me.*

BEING PERPETUALLY CURIOUS, we want to know what is over the next hill, around the bend in the river, or on the other side of the universe. From infancy on, we explore our world, looking with awe and wonder at all we see, forever seeking to understand it better. Indeed, one way of reviewing human history is to examine our exploration of the created order.

Our curiosity about and explorations of the universe leave us with countless questions: How did all this come into existence? What force holds the universe together? What makes the sun rise and set each day? Where do comets come from and where do they go? What causes the rain and the snow? What makes a flag flap in the breeze? We turn to astronomers, physicists, chemists, and scientists of all stripes for answers, answers that sometimes satisfy our curiosity and other times lead to even more questions.

We look inward with the same curiosity. What causes new life to come into existence? Why do we get sick? What causes the different pigmentations and physical features of various peoples? What is love? How do we acquire our emotions? What causes death? What happens after we die? Again, the questions are limitless, and this time we turn also to philosophers, theologians, and storytellers for explanations and insight.

We demand answers to satisfy our boundless curiosity. Sometimes we find a logical, rational, or scientific answer, but more often than not, one answer leads to more questions and deeper exploration. As we continue probing and searching, we come to the question of all questions: *Who?* It is no longer a matter of asking, "Why was the universe, seen and unseen, created?" or even, "What force created it and sustains it?" but, "*Who* did it and *who* is doing it?" To my mind the only plausible answer is that an entity exists that is far more powerful than any single person or even the sum total of all humans through the ages. We have finally come first to suspect and then to believe that some unknown and far greater and more powerful being than us is at work in our world.

Our ancestors came to call that entity "god." They believed in a god or goddess who created all things and brought all things, both seen and unseen, into existence. Almost every clan, tribe, or nation has come to believe in some creator deity endowed with supreme powers. Although each culture had its own name for this god and identified what it perceived to be this god's unique attributes, all cultures were united in the belief that such a creator deity existed.

6

But surely, they reasoned, to maintain everything we humans can perceive and experience must be too great a task for a single god or goddess. Eventually they concluded that there must be lesser, subservient deities who took responsibilities for various aspects of life. Thus, it came about that our ancient ancestors, in their quest to understand the universe, developed numerous myths, legends, and sagas about these powerful beings. They believed that one god was responsible for the sun, another for the rain, still another took charge of fertility, and other gods assumed responsibility for death and the afterlife, and so on. In their polytheistic way of thinking, there was a god or goddess for everything, and everything had a deity. When new things were discovered and identified, whether it was a new astronomical phenomenon or something as simple as a toothache, it could only mean that a new deity had either come into existence or was, at long last, revealing his or her presence to the people.

Each deity was given a name, and gradually the people began observing and then interpreting the actions of their gods, creating stories about them in an effort to better understand their attributes. These stories were passed down from one generation to the next, first as part of the oral and pictoral traditions and then the written traditions of their culture. Some gods were kind and benevolent; others were arrogant, abusive, and destructive. Some gods brought about new life; others destroyed it. Some gods were powerful; others were limited in what they could do. Some were passionately concerned about human welfare; others were capricious, playful, teasing, or mean spirited. As the personality of each deity was discerned, people realized the necessity of making appropriate responses to their gods in order to secure their blessing or to prevent incurring their wrath.

To discover or to be told the name of a god was supremely important, for to be able to call on the name of the god gave humans access to divine powers. Indeed, to know a god's name gave some measure of human control over that deity, for then the god could be summoned to perform some extraordinary or powerful deed. Perhaps the most popularly known example of this is the Arabian story of Aladdin and his magic lamp, which housed a powerful genie—a lesser but still powerful deity. Whenever Aladdin rubbed the lamp and summoned the genie, he could order the genie to perform heroic feats on his behalf. In some cultures all the people knew the names of their gods; in other cultures only the priests and priestesses were granted that knowledge, and in those cases, the priests and priestesses had great power over both the rulers and their subjects.

7

In addition to the gods that an individual and family might worship on their own, corporate cultic worship began to take on an increasingly important role in the life of the individual, as well as in the clan, tribe, or nation. Worship became more organized and regulated, normally under the guidance and leadership of a priest or priestess who was recognized as having extraordinary access to the deity. Only those individuals had the secret knowledge and training that gave them special insight into what pleased or displeased the gods. Only they knew how to "read the signs," to interpret the will of the gods to the people, or to prophesy what the gods would do on their behalf. Thus, when a farmer prepared to plant his crops or a woman hoped to conceive a child, these leaders made their supplications to the fertility god or goddess for divine blessings. Similarly, if drought had left a region parched, if a severe storm threatened to harm them, if there was a plague, or if anything bad was happening to the people, surely, they reasoned, it must be because the gods were angry with them and punishing them. Only the priest or priestess could stand before the altars in the temples and shrines and make the proper invocations to appease their anger.

It was not always sufficient to merely ask the deity for a successful growing season, a healthy child, victory in battle, relief from desperate situations, or other favors. An offering also had to be made to secure the god's favor or to avert her or his wrath, and typically the nature of the required sacrifice was codified or was the particular knowledge of the priest or priestess. Depending on what the supplicant had requested of the god or the severity of the offense against the deity, it might require an offering of farm produce, livestock, gold, silver, precious stones, or even a human life.

As nations and societies became more developed and structured, the role of the priests and priestesses took on increasing significance. Before a ruler went to war, he needed to know whether his campaign would be blessed or cursed by his nation's war god. To secure success on the battlefield, he would offer a sacrifice on behalf of his soldiers and subjects. If he was victorious, upon his return he would make additional sacrifices of thanksgiving. When a new ruler took power, he offered his prayers and sacrifices to the appropriate gods so his reign might be long and his people would prosper. But here, too, only the priest or priestess had the hidden knowledge of what was necessary. Little surprise, then, that in some cultures, the power of the priests began to surpass that of the ruler, especially if the ruler was deemed weak. Even in the best of circumstances, a strong rivalry for supremacy existed between the ruler and the priests.

In other cultures, such as in ancient Egypt, for many centuries the rulers (pharaohs) assumed the dual role of secular and spiritual leader. It was the pharaoh's sacred responsibility to lead public prayers and make sacrifices to the sun god each morning, and to lead the public worship at the shrines of the fertility goddesses before the planting season. Priests and priestesses, along with many court officials, lived and served at the temples of the lesser gods and goddesses, the better to make their own supplications. However, because the pharaoh served as the nation's chief priest before the gods, he was recognized as the living embodiment of the deities.

It was inevitable that the various tribes and nations of the Near Middle East would confront one another in war. Prior to a military campaign, both warring nations prayed and sacrificed to their war gods to ensure victory on the battlefield, yet there was always a victor and a loser. But how could this be, the people wondered. If both sides prayed to their gods and made all the right sacrifices, if all the signs were positive, if they had their god's favor, then how could one side win and the other lose? They came to realize that one nation's war god may be stronger than their opponent's war god. Just as human armies waged war on the battlefield on earth, they reasoned that their gods also waged war in the heavens. If one god defeated his opponent, the devotees of the victorious god would win on the battlefield. If the losing army and people were put to the sword or taken into captivity and eventually assimilated into the victorious side's culture, it meant that their god had been killed and no longer existed. Or, if one army was defeated but managed to retreat to fight another day, it was taken to mean that their war god had been wounded in battle, needed to recover, and would make another attempt at victory.

9

The power of the deities had yet another limitation. It was commonly held that a god or goddess was limited by the geography on earth. If a merchant traveled from Ur in

Mesopotamia to Thebes in Egypt, he feared that as soon as he left the Chaldean territory, he also left his god's protection. Only the strongest and most powerful deities could transcend geographical limitations. Little wonder that the enslaved Israelites seriously doubted whether the God of Abraham, Isaac, and Jacob could help them in Egypt. They had prayed and sacrificed to God for years, but nothing had happened. And when they looked at the ten plagues worked by Moses in an attempt to secure their release, their doubts only increased. Moses might have done mighty deeds, but each deed was countered by an equal or even greater deed done by the Egyptian priests. Perhaps, they reasoned, the God of their ancestors was powerless in Egypt.

This polytheistic world must have been a terrifying place for people. So many different gods and goddesses needed to be placated, addressed, and honored that the people perpetually feared that somewhere in the heavens or on earth lurked yet another god who was angry because he had been ignored. That god might be the very one causing all their troubles, or, conversely, might be the very one who could grant them the fulfillment of their particular prayers.

The first known attempt of establishing monotheism (the worship of one god) in the Western world came during the reign of Egyptian pharaoh Akenaton (1379–1362 BC), when he made the radical proclamation that there was only one god, Aton. After centuries of worshipping a pantheon of deities, his subjects were commanded to join him and his wife, Nefertiti, in worshipping this one god. All other gods and goddesses were declared to be false, and the people were forbidden to worship them. He angered the priests and priestesses by closing their temples at Thebes and elsewhere and moving the center of government and cultic worship to the new city of Amon. There, in the desert along the Nile River, he built a new capital, complete with numerous temples, shrines, palaces, and living quarters for over twenty thousand people.

This foray into monotheism ended with Akenaton's death. Almost immediately the old temples were reopened and the priests resumed their duties, with more power than ever, and they quickly took revenge by having the late pharaoh's name excised from all monuments. The boy king Tutankhamen was enthroned, and his stepmother, Nefertiti, seemingly disappeared from public life. The new city of Amon was razed and abandoned. Within a short time, polytheism was firmly re-established throughout Egypt and its colonies.

What is astounding is that monotheism survived at all. It did so through Abram, a citizen of Ur of the Chaldeans. Although we know little about his background, we do know that he grew up in a polytheistic culture—until his unique encounter with the deity we have since come to identify and worship as God. Either by choice or because he was forced to leave his ancestral home, Abram and his extended family migrated into the land of the Canaanites, in what is present-day Israel. There, amid several polytheistic cultures, he began establishing monotheism.

The Book of Genesis tells the long saga of Abram, or Abraham as God renamed him because of his faithful obedience, and how his descendants prospered until a terrible famine swept over the land and forced them to migrate to Egypt's Nile delta. There, for the next four hundred years, they remained a distinct culture and, at least for a time, flourished in that alien land. More than anything else, it was their refusal to be absorbed and assimilated into Egyptian culture that created many of their hardships. The general practice in Egypt at the time was for anyone who embraced the Egyptian ethos, culture, and worship patterns, regardless of their race or place of origin, to be deemed an Egyptian. That was the one thing the descendants of Abraham steadfastly refused to do. They would not worship the Egyptian gods and, from what little we can glean from the Bible, rarely intermarried, choosing to remain a distinct people. After several hundred years, they had worn out their welcome.

The writers of Genesis note that a new administration enslaved the Israelites during a seven-year famine. That makes for great drama, but it is something of a misleading statement, for in Egyptian culture, the pharaoh, as the

11

human representative of the gods, at least theoretically owned everyone and everything in his empire, including all native-born Egyptians. During this famine the people had become so desperate for food that they willingly traded first their livestock, then all their personal possessions, and finally themselves for something to eat, thereby formalizing their status as slaves. The Israelites were no exception. However, because they continued to refuse to identify themselves with Egyptian culture, and refused to acknowledge the pharaoh as a living god, they were more harshly treated than others. They chafed at their enslavement and sought to return to the freedom of their homeland.

Firmly believing in the divine right of absolute power, the pharaoh had no desire to part with any of his human chattel. The Israelites, like others living in the pharaoh's land, labored for several months each year on his public work projects and were forced to pay a substantial tax to the government. To allow them to leave simply because they were unhappy living under his rule would have been economically detrimental. It potentially could also have led to a general uprising of other unhappy subjects throughout the country.

12

Hearing the complaints of his people, God raised up Moses, who, after working a number of great miracles on his behalf, finally secured the freedom of the Israelites. On the morning following the first Passover, they fled Egypt, crossed the sea, and entered into the Sinai desert. There they remained for the next forty years before finally being allowed to cross the Jordan River back into the land of their ancestors. Why the long delay?

The distance between Egypt and Israel is relatively short, and for centuries camel caravans had traversed the region in weeks or days. Even though it would have taken much longer for such a large group of people and their livestock to make the journey, it would not have taken them anywhere near forty years. Perhaps we would be wiser to consider this forty years in light of Jewish numerology: The journey took the "fullness of time," or the complete time necessary. In the course of the two Testaments, we see this number forty taking on symbolic significance for both Jews and Christians. So they wander for forty years, a period that the writers of the Book of Exodus ascribe to the people having sinned against their Lord God. That is the punishment for those who had once been enslaved in Egypt. They were denied the privilege of entering into the Promised Land—yet. That much is true, but it is only part of the story.

Quite simply, the Israelites needed this time to rid themselves of several hundred years of Egyptian culture and theology, to cease thinking like slaves of the pharaoh and to develop a new cultural identity before they entered into and then dispersed throughout the Promised Land. The time in the wilderness can be compared to a military boot camp: new recruits are taken to a completely strange and frighteningly mysterious destination. Upon their arrival the drill instructors begin stripping them of their old civil ways and identities, replacing those with a military identity and indoctrinating them with the ethos and lifestyle of a soldier. And so it was for the Israelites in the wilderness. They had to understand their new identity: who and whose they were.

13

The new sense of identity came with the basic affirmation and embrace of monotheism, a better understanding of the nature of their God and what was expected of the people as found in the first commandment: I am the Lord your God; you shall have no other gods but me.

This commandment does not say that there are no other gods or goddesses. Indeed, the statement is completely and tantalizingly neutral as to their possible existence. Whether or not there are other deities is immaterial—these people are to worship only God.

At the outset this commandment appears to be very simple and straightforward, as indeed it is in certain ways. One would think it would be the easiest command to obey because the supremacy and sanctity of absolute monotheism are clearly stated, and the people are instructed in no uncertain terms that they are to worship only the Lord God, or, to use the ancient cultic formula, "the God of Abraham, Isaac, and Jacob." At least in theory, this commandment should have come as a great relief to the

Israelites because they now had only one deity to worship instead of having to attempt to placate a multitude. Yet, the reality was radically different; almost from the moment the people received this law, they began violating it. There are several reasons why this occurred.

First, as we shall explore in greater detail with the third commandment, when Moses had initially encountered the Lord God at the burning bush, he wanted to know God's name, but God refused to reveal it. Instead, God obliquely replied, "I AM WHO I AM." In other words, God was not going to allow Moses to know God's proper name. This meant that Moses could not conjure up God at will, nor force God to reveal the secret phrases that would ensure God would do his bidding. It meant God was not diminishing or sharing any of his authority, power, or autonomy with mere mortals, nor would God allow himself to be controlled by them. God was, and would remain, all powerful. It also meant that by not revealing his name, God was not fully disclosing all his attributes at one time but could continue to express and reveal himself to the people as they were ready to receive it. From the start it meant that a relationship with God could never be static. It was also God's way of telling Moses, "That is none of your business."

◆
14

To know the name of a person, and more so of a deity, gives one power over that person or deity. For example, if I am walking down the street and see my friend John ahead of me, I can shout out his name, and if he hears it, even if he doesn't recognize my voice, he will invariably turn around to see who is calling him. That may seem like a small measure of control, but it is control because I have made him do something he might not have done otherwise. Further, to know the name of a person or a deity is to have some understanding of his nature, personality, and attributes. It also means that I can categorize him, label him. For example, if several of us get together and mention the name of an absent mutual friend, Charlie, we don't have to describe what he looks like, his personality, what he does, or anything else. We don't even have to define our relationship with Charlie. We "know" not only who we are discussing but many things about him.

So it is with God. Because Moses and the Israelites were not permitted to know God's proper name, they could not immediately discern all his attributes, much less categorize and label him. That was precisely what God wanted, but it was very disconcerting to the people. Only gradually, first through the Ten Commandments and later through more intimate personal and corporate experiences, would they come to understand what God was like and what God required of them. Because they were unable to carve from stone or wood a tangible symbol that represented God and therefore could not pray or sacrifice before a material representation of their God, they had to enter into a completely spiritual relationship with God. Even centuries later, both Jesus and the writers of the Epistles had a difficult time explaining to their followers that God is spirit and must be worshipped in the spiritual sense, not with tangible idols.

This was a unique form of worship, almost totally different from anything they or anyone else of that era and part of the world had ever experienced. How, then, were they to know and understand a deity who had no apparent shape or form? Predominantly masculine titles and terms have traditionally been used to describe God because the people lived in a patriarchal society and often transferred to God their own assumptions and prejudices. But was God indeed male or female, or both, or neither? If God does not take shape or form but is revealed in burning bushes, clouds, or the "still small voice," how can one know that God exists except through ecstatic or spiritual encounters? With all these unanswerable questions, it is not surprising that the people initially had doubts about the existence of God as well as about God's claims to universal and supreme powers, and therefore often flirted with other deities.

15

The second reason the Israelites found it so difficult to faithfully obey this commandment was that all their neighboring tribes, nations, and empires were polytheistic. Rather than interpret their call to strict monotheism as a tremendous blessing, they saw themselves as sorely deprived. They knew their God to be a mighty warrior, as evidenced by the Passover and the Exodus, but repeatedly in the wilderness, they demanded to know of Moses if God could provide them with their material needs of food, water, clothing, shelter, and fertility. Could one deity really be both a war god and a provider of the things they needed for survival? It seemed like too much to ask, much less expect. Considering that they had so recently escaped from a powerful polytheistic empire and were still surrounded by other polytheists, it is of little surprise that their initial trust in the absolute supremacy of this one God was so low. Yet, it was this very matter of complete trust and faith in God that was of paramount importance. Everything else in their relationship with God depended on it.

The covenant between God and the Israelites was the cornerstone of their national life and ethos, and it gave them a sense of identity both as a nation and as individuals. The relationship was straightforward: If the people remained faithful in worshipping only God, they would be blessed and enjoy success in every endeavor. Conversely, if they became unfaithful by not worshipping God exclusively, they would be punished and suffer greatly.

16

The rest of the Old Testament can be seen as a centuries-long history of how the Israelites obeyed or disobeyed this commandment. For example, nearly all the judges during the confederation of the tribes, and the kings during the monarchical era, were deemed to be either good or evil not because of their wisdom, public policies, or military victories, but solely in light of their obedience to the first commandment. Nothing else seemed to matter to the writers. Thus, Gideon was proclaimed to be a good Judge because he was a strict monotheist full of zeal for God, even though he took unnecessary risks on the battlefield. Samson, despite all his personal failings, became a hero because of his zeal. David and Hezekiah were "good" kings despite their character flaws; Ahab and Queen Jezebel, on the other hand, were "wicked" and "evil" because they were not zealous for God, and even promoted the worship of foreign gods.

Though contemporary Christians understand that they are to remain loyal to God, they are also keenly aware of their numerous shortcomings and times of failure. Choices abound in our age, where technology constantly changes but the human heart does not. Today it is possible to learn, explore, and experience firsthand other religions and philosophies that were previously inaccessible to us. For example, at the very time Moses was leading the Israelites out of Egypt, Hinduism was already well established in India, but India was so far away that it might as well have been on the dark side of the moon. Even if the Israelites knew of its existence, it would be centuries before anyone from the Middle East traveled there to explore a different religion, then returned home to introduce it to his own people. By contrast, now we can visit India in less than a day's travel by air to learn about Hinduism firsthand; we can visit a Sikh community right in our own neigborhood; and we can study Hinduism via books, the Internet, or other forms of media.

Though two centuries of immigration to North America have brought millions of adherents of other faiths to these shores, the first wave of new immigrants was primarily Christians from Europe—Congregationalists who settled in New England, Anglicans in Virginia. At first attempts were made to establish an Old Testament–style theocracy in both areas. The leaders of the little settlement at Plymouth spoke of their land as being the New Jerusalem, the New Zion, the City Set on a Hill that was to be a beacon of light to the enslaved Europeans still languishing under Anglicanism or Roman Catholicism. Possession of the Anglican Book of Common Prayer in the Massachusetts Bay Colony was a capital offense, and when Roger Williams expressed what others took to be heresy about the right of freedom of worship, he was "hived out" (i.e., banished) to what is now Rhode Island. In Virginia, only Anglicans could vote or hold office, and those convicted of being Quakers were in danger of forfeiting their lives. Since then millions of immigrants of other faiths, or with no specific faith at all, have settled in the United States, each adding their own contribution to our overall understanding of this commandment and its applications and implications.

17

Even though the majority of the signers of the Declaration of Independence and the writers of the

Constitution were Protestant churchmen, they intentionally chose to forbid the establishment of a national Church. This new country did not even proclaim itself to be a "Christian nation," even though the majority of its citizens were at least nominal Christians. This was disconcerting to many churchmen and churchwomen who believed that this country had been uniquely blessed by God and had a divine mandate to be the new Holy Land. Various political and religious groups in the past have attempted to make the United States into a Christian nation. In the nineteenth century, a small third political party, the Know Nothings, arose in an attempt to suppress what their constituents thought was a danger to Protestantism from Roman Catholics, Mormons, Masons, and other non-Protestant groups. From the 1970s to the end of the twentieth century, a loose coalition of conservatives, composed primarily of Republicans and evangelical Protestants, created what has become known as the New Christian Right. Its goals are to make the country more conservative politically, to reverse what they believe to be liberal and anti-Christian decisions by the Supreme Court, to support Israel in its conflict with the Palestinians, and to make this into the "Christian" nation that they understand was envisioned by the Pilgrims who settled New England.

One reason these more conservative groups have worked so hard to achieve their goals is that they do not like much of what they see. Until fairly recently, many universities, professional schools, resorts and recreational areas, and even some entire communities had unwritten policies of admitting only white Protestants to their midst. To its shame, the resort and artist community where I live, Saugatuck, Michigan, once had a sign on the city limits proclaiming it to be a "White Gentile Village." Just a few miles to the north, in the city of Holland, restrictive real estate covenants once forbade selling property to Roman Catholics or non-Christians. Fortunately, such blatant forms of discrimination are now against the law.

The old traditions have changed. In addition to Christian places of worship, almost every community has at least one small mosque, synagogue, or temples of worship for

Hindus, Buddhists, and others, and accommodation is given to those who choose to be devout atheists. These are the very things that make obedience to and fulfillment of this commandment so challenging for many Christians. If the land had been dedicated to God and deemed to be protected by God's blessing, how can toleration and accommodation be given to those who are not zealous in their worship of God? It is little wonder that many "hot Gospel" sermons are preached each week, with the dire warning that unless America "gets back to God," God will turn his wrath on this nation, just as God did to the ancient Israelites.

Even for more moderate Christians, who have no desire to close non-Christian places of worship, deport non-Christians, or discriminate or perpetuate violence against them, religious tolerance remains a challenge. How far are we to go as individuals, as Churches, and as a nation in tolerating those who do not share similar beliefs or make similar professions of faith? What are the limits? Indeed, are there, or should there be, any limits?

There are no easy answers to those questions, and we find ourselves forced to work out our own answers. Perhaps we are even forced to find our own questions. No wonder some individuals find it easier to retreat to their own interpetation of orthodoxy, relying on traditions from the past. Some find it far easier to attack and accuse others of heresy, zealously claiming that they alone hold a monopoly on the truth. I am convinced that a far better way is to follow the advice of Paul, working out our own salvation with prayer and discernment rather than shredding the ideas or practices of others. We would do well to remember that we are on a spiritual journey ourselves and have our own challenges to face, explore, and study.

The second contemporary challenge for Christians seeking to obey the first commandment is "civil religion." Almost any political, social, or economic system, whether it is capitalism, patriotism, patriarchalism, fascism, socialism, racism, and so on, has the potential to become a civil, or secular, form of religion. Because they are not "spiritual" in the traditional sense, they are even more dangerous

◆

because they can be so insidious. They often use many of the same forms of liturgy as traditional religion: They rely on sacred icons and holy places and demand the complete loyalty of their followers.

Let us use patriotism as an example. In its most base and arrogant form, it encourages its adherents to smugly believe, "I am a patriotic American, therefore I am saved." As adherents look around them, they can see sufficient evidence to support the veracity of their belief. There is an abundance of churches and places of worship that signify a freedom of worship, a constitutional government based on laws rather than the mere whims of a leader, a strong tradition of civil rights, and great wealth and educational opportunities unknown in many other nations in the world. We are, we insist, a God-fearing people because the Pledge of Allegiance says we are "one nation under God," and on our currency we have the logo "In God We Trust." Surely, they reason, having all those things and more is a clear sign of God's blessing on this country, a sign that Americans are a chosen people. In turn, adherents of such beliefs understand themselves as having a divinely decreed responsibility to promote American values and virtues to the rest of the world.

This sometimes leads to a strong sentiment that is suggested, even bellowed: One cannot be a true American Christian unless one is also sufficiently zealous as a patriot, and one cannot be a true American patriot without also being a strong and zealous Christian. For better or for worse, the terms are seldom expansively defined, and even those who are self-proclaimed patriots and zealous Christians would not always agree on the definition. Rather, what holds these beliefs together is a "feeling" that is all too often exclusive of those who do not hold the same values. Interestingly, other nations, such as Canada just to the north, rarely find it necessary to blend religious beliefs with public patriotic events.

With almost evangelical fervor, from the time of the Pilgrims on, we have attempted to take this message to the rest of the world, seeing ourselves as a spiritual beacon with the divine mandate to enlighten the rest of the world. More recently, as America has become increasingly involved in international affairs, first during the tenure of Theodore Roosevelt, through both World Wars, in the "gunboat diplomacy" of the last century, and in Korea, Vietnam, Grenada, and the Persian Gulf, we have promoted American beliefs, sometimes at bayonet point, in defense of our self-proclaimed interests. We have also done it in more peaceful ways, most notably through the Peace Corps. The United States Information Agency motto encapsulates the ethos: "Telling America's Story to the World."

People of all nations take pride in the accomplishments of their country and its citizens, in their resources and their cultural traditions. Few, however, do so with the same enthusiasm as do many Americans. Indeed, we can hardly imagine any other nation, for example, the Canadians, making such audacious claims because this type of civil religion is unique to the United States, and therefore offensive to much of the rest of the world. What makes this form of civil religion so dangerous is that it blends political theory and patriotism with Christian forms of worship.

◆
21

Another way we can violate the first commandment is by making a tangible or intangible thing into our god. We do it with athletes, entertainers, age (primarily youth), physical beauty, and the whole concept of "celebrity." We do it with our money, referring to it as the "almighty dollar," and by building our banks in the style of ancient Greek temples. The implication is clear: We worship the power and strength of money, making our offerings and petitions for special favors to our money managers, carefully listening to the latest oracle from the chairman of the Federal Reserve, or studying the holy writ of the Dow Jones.

That type of civil or secular religion is an insidious challenge because we often do not see it as a type of religion, much less as competition for our relationship with God. The reason is simple: We have compartmentalized our lives. It is almost as if we say, "Sunday mornings I will devote to church; Sunday afternoon is for sports. On Monday through Friday, I am at work, supporting the capitalist system. Tuesday night is my lodge night. Thursday evening I become a patriot when I attend a political rally. Friday night I am a hedonist or an epicurean when we go out for dinner and a night on the town."

When we think of civil religion in those terms, we see that that is what the ancient Israelites were attempting to do through much of their long history. They began by interpreting God primarily as a war god, compartmentalizing God, turning to God whenever they saw a military danger to their security. At other times they resorted to the Baal gods, believing that those deities could provide for their other needs. It was idolatry for them, and it is for us, too, when we compartmentalize our lives instead of making all that we do and say an offering to God. That sort of compartmentalization is egotism run rampant; someone has suggested that ego is an acronym for "edging God out."

As an Episcopalian, I have an additional challenge in keeping this commandment. Because of our denomination's long history, our ethos and traditions, it is incredibly easy to make our worship into a type of deity, focusing our attention on who we are and what we are doing rather than on God. We can be more concerned about keeping cadence with the liturgy or our "liturgical aerobics" rather than the intentions and worship behind our standing, sitting, and kneeling.

Keeping this commandment is a continual battle for us. Fortunately, we do have a clear example of perfect obedience in Jesus Christ. After spending forty days in the wilderness following his baptism by John, Jesus was tempted three times. In each case he was offered the chance to sell his soul for something created—bread, power, and the accolades of the crowds. Nothing is inherently wrong with those things. Indeed, we need all of them for our survival as whole persons. But as Jesus considered those temptations, he realized their cost. To have yielded to them would have been far too expensive because they would have come between himself and God. Rather than advancing Jesus' ministry, they would have interrupted it, taken precedence over it.

22

In all things that appeal to our senses or our mind, we must follow Jesus' example: Will embracing something separate us from Christ or bring us closer to him? Whatever leads us away and separates us from God is a potential idol and false deity. Let us draw close to God.

◆

G. Corwin Stoppel

CHAPTER TWO

✦

Embracing a Complex God

THE SECOND COMMANDMENT

You shall make no graven image.

LMOST EVERY CHILD ASKS, "What does God look like?"
It is a child's question, but it is far from being
childish.

How utterly frustrating it must have been for the
Israelites, still traveling slowly through the wilderness, to
have been told that they could not and would not have a
physical, tangible representation of their God before them
when they worshipped. In Egypt they had been surrounded
by the idols of the various gods and goddesses. But when
Moses came down from the mountain with the stone
tablets of the Ten Commandments, he told them they
would not be allowed to create representations of the deity.
It had been frustrating enough to learn that they were to
worship only one deity, but now they were not even allowed
to see what God looked like. How were they to know what
God was like without some physical or tangible representation of God? What would be their focal point when they
prayed, worshipped, or made sacrifices?

Since prehistoric times, as men and women began iden-
tifying and understanding the nature of the gods and goddesses that they believed ruled their world, they created for
themselves symbols of the deities, endowing them with
appropriate attributes. Thus, a fertility deity was often

depicted as a very pregnant woman with large breasts and wide hips, or as a well-endowed male. A war god might be shown to have strong muscles and an idealistic image of a warrior's body and fierce demeanor. To represent these gods, people sometimes chose birds of prey because of their great speed, wild animals because of their strength and courage, or mythical creatures. Sometimes the idols were half animal and half human.

For the most part, people understood that idols were not the actual gods but served as a tangible representation. Only a few individuals and smaller cultures believed that the objects they had fashioned of wood, stone, or metal were actually gods. Far more typically, the people believed the idols became sacred objects because they represented the gods and could serve as a focal point for worship and sacrifice. Thus, to lay offerings before idols, to bow down and pray before them, or to make sacrifices at their altars became a visible means of demonstrating devotion to the gods themselves. Perhaps one way of understanding this as Christians is to remember what Jesus told his followers: Give so much as a drink of cold water to someone in need, welcome even the youngest child, and it is as if you are doing it for (and to) me.

Precisely because the idols represented their gods, the devotees lavished great attention and care on them. The more powerful and important the god was to their welfare, the more elaborate her or his statue, altar, or shrine would be. The more the people believed in the potency of a particular god, the more they sought to honor her or him by contributing precious metals, gemstones, or other expensive and rare gifts. It was not uncommon for an altar to be laden with goods at a time when the people were starving, or for an idol to be decorated with the gold the people could have used to buy the things they needed for their basic survival.

The priests and priestesses who served in the temples and at the shrines had an especially close relationship with the deities and were themselves considered to be holy men and women. As such they were allowed to enjoy some of the benefits of the contributions and sacrifices made by the people. For example, if a devotee brought grain, fruit, or meat to sacrifice to the gods, once the ritual had been completed, the priests were allowed to keep a portion for themselves. Among the Greeks and Romans, it was not uncommon for a shrine or temple to operate a market or butcher shop, where excess contributions were sold to the public and the proceeds used for the financial support of the temple. (That is why Paul, in his letter to the Corinthians, writes about meat being sacrificed to false idols.) The system was ripe for abuse, for the priests believed it was their prerogative, if not responsibility, to keep the sacrifices for their own use rather than share them with others. During times of famine, they might continue to eat very well while the people were starving; they might be dressed in sumptuous garments while the people wore threadbare rags.

This reverence for idols that represent the gods should not seem so strange or remote to us, for we often display similar tendencies. The difference is that many of the things we most respect are tangible symbols of some very secular deities. For example, the red, green, and amber of a traffic light not only instruct motorists and pedestrians what to do but also become a symbol of law and order. Intentionally driving through a red light is not just danger-ous to all others at the intersection but demonstrates a fla-grant disregard for a particular law, and by extension, the entire ethos of law and order. Or, the American flag, with its stars and stripes, is, in reality, only a multicolored piece of cloth, but it is treated with tremendous respect and ritual, almost reverence, by many people because it symbolizes the ethos and recent history of at least some of the citizens of the United States. To honor and treat the flag with respect symbolizes loyalty and patriotism to the country, and honor and dignity to those who sacrificed their lives for freedom and peace. Conversely, to burn the flag in protest, to trample it underfoot, or to use it in an inappro-priate way are vivid means of showing contempt for the country, not just the flag. Similarly, the Confederate flag is not just a reminder of a past era; for many it symbolizes the

◆

27

concept of states' rights or even segregation and slavery. Indeed, some use this ancient battle flag as a taunting symbol of their rejection of integration, a strong central government, or anything else they deem too modern or too liberal. As Christians we treat the Bible (Latin for "collection of books") with extraordinary respect, and even designate it the "Holy Bible," to signify that it is different from all other books because it contains the word of God between its covers. We may allow our Bibles to go unread and collect dust, but most of us would have second thoughts about casually tossing even a well-worn one into the trash bin.

We use a variety of symbols in our life, and give some of them semisacred status. A balanced scale represents equal justice and fairness for all and righteous justice. A stick with a snake entwined around it symbolizes the medical profession. Commercial and military pilots proudly wear wings on their uniforms to represent their professional achievement and responsibility, and in return expect to be respected and obeyed by passengers and flight crews. In the military, different insignia represent different ranks; a ring worn on the third finger of the left hand symbolizes the wearer's marriage vows.

28

For a time during China's cultural revolution, a concerted effort was made to purge the country and the military of all symbols that marked a difference between people. Everyone was encouraged to wear the same drab green uniform, and in the military, all insignia were removed. It was an interesting concept, but it soon proved unworkable. Soldiers could not identify their officers, so on an unsanctioned and informal basis, junior officers began carrying one ballpoint pen in their breast pocket; senior officers, two. The idea of not displaying rank was soon abandoned!

On a more personal level, individuals and families often treasure heirlooms and photographs handed down from one generation to another. Even if the objects have little or no intrinsic value to anyone else, they are deemed priceless by the owner solely because of what they represent. A badly cracked piece of pottery that someone else might throw into the garbage might be prominently displayed because it belonged to a long-deceased relative who carried it west in a covered wagon. Photographs are carefully preserved because they are the tangible symbols of special moments or people in our lives. After a fire or some other disaster, even if they have lost everything else, survivors often express gratitude that they were at least able to save the family pictures.

All these things, unless we are careful, can be treated with such great respect that they become our deities, our focal points of work, sacrifice, and prayer. The difficulty is not with the symbols themselves but with how we treat them. We violate this commandment when we begin to worship these objects as sacred things in themselves. Such symbols can stop us from growing, from experiencing new things, and from moving on in life, because objects are static and force us to remain emotionally, spiritually, and sometimes even physically frozen in place.

For example, a man was married for many years, and then his wife died. In their home were many pictures of them together and some portraits of her alone. In time he sufficiently recovers from his grief so that he is ready to enter into a new relationship when friends introduce him to another woman. They spend time together, and even though he is starting to grow to love her, he refuses to remove his wedding ring or take down his wife's pictures. By keeping those things prominently in place, he is effectively worshipping the past and announcing that he is not ready to move forward. Under those circumstances, it is highly doubtful he will move on in life.

29

Or, decades ago my grandmother took to a church dinner a serving dish that had once belonged to her mother. Another woman was helping in the kitchen, and she accidentally broke it. That was the last time Grandmother spoke to that woman, clearly implying that the dish and the memories associated with it meant more to her than the friendship with the other woman.

We also make idols of intangible things such as social position, personal pride, political power, personality, intellect or anti-intellectualism, and even our emotions. Some people are so filled with high self-esteem that they become incensed whenever they feel slighted by anyone who does not immediately recognize their attributes. Some have literally made a deity of their anger, depression, or cheerfulness. Others take inordinate pride in being "self-made" individuals, ones who had little or no formal education and yet accomplished much—and insist on being constantly recognized for what they have achieved. Still others take tremendous pride in belonging to organizations composed exclusively of those whose ancestors arrived before nationhood, or who fought in the Revolutionary War or the Civil War. We have seen it happen with momentous events in our personal or corporate life, too. For two individuals it might be the day they first met, became engaged, married, or gave birth to their first child. For a nation it might be a historic date such as July 4, 1776; the beginning or end of the Civil War; December 7, 1941; D-Day on June 6, 1944; the end of World War II; or more recently September 11, 2001.

Unless we are careful, we can make anything into a deity and squeeze out God.

◆

For that reason God refuses to be symbolized by an object. There are to be no images depicting his attributes or powers, or giving an artist's representation of his appearance. God is too big, complex, multidimensional, and powerful to be locked into a single idol or one tangible symbol. Had the Israelites been allowed to create a statue or another image of God, before long they would have limited themselves to seeing God only in that fashion. Because their first encounter with God had been as a war god who defeated the Egyptians, their idols and statues would have reflected that, and it would have been difficult for them to grow in their relationship with God. When we compare early Judaism with other religions, we immediately see the difference: Greco-Roman culture began depicting Hermes/Mercury as a messenger god and nothing else, Venus as a fertility goddess and nothing else, and so forth.

We have seen this happen in Christianity, too. When Michelangelo was commissioned to paint the ceiling of the Sistine Chapel, he created a magnificent mural of the creation of humanity. God is depicted as an elderly white male with a long, flowing beard, extending a hand to give life to

Adam. For many sincere, devout Christians, God is forever imagined that way.

We have also seen it happen in our use of language. Because the ancient Israelites, like most of the other cultures in the Middle East at that time, were paternalistic, the masculine and militaristic side of God traditionally has been emphasized. Only in the past few decades have we begun to more carefully explore the nurturing, loving, and more feminine sides of God's nature. Some favor this "new" way of looking at the attributes of God (though in reality such images pervade Scripture), but others believe that even to consider the feminine aspects of God is blasphemous. The latter may very well have made an idol of the masculine language and attributes of God.

We have seen it in our depiction of Jesus. There are, of course, no photographs or drawings of Jesus from his time on earth, so artists have taken the liberty of painting him in their own likeness. In our Western culture, Jesus is predominantly depicted as having Nordic features with a deep suntan. It came as a rude shock to many Westerners when they first saw African and Asian art depicting Jesus with non-Nordic features. Just as with the exploration of new language to describe God, the idea of a nonwhite, non-blonde Jesus seemed to some to be sheer blasphemy. That was made real for me when I was growing up in a small town in Minnesota in the 1960s, and our Sunday school teacher first showed us African images of Jesus. It simply had never occurred to us that he could look like anything other than someone who had just stepped off the boat from Scandinavia.

As we explore language and images, we begin to see the real challenge of idolatry, and the difficulty in keeping this commandment. We are tempted to limit God and Jesus Christ to our own experiences and points of reference. Yet in doing so, we have put God and Jesus in a box of our own making, and we feel highly agitated whenever a different way of understanding or imagining God or Jesus is revealed to us. Obedience to this commandment means we must intentionally choose to worship God and not the created.

G. Corwin Stoppel

Thus, we measure what we say and do against whether it leads to a true worship of God or to some form of idolatry.

In the longer version of this commandment, we are enjoined against creating a likeness of anything on the planet, in the water, or in the sky or the heavens above. After exploring the ease with which we can worship the created things rather than the Creator, we can more easily understand why God would give this instruction to the Israelites while they were still in the wilderness. At the very time Moses was receiving the Ten Commandments, Aaron and some of the leaders of the people were melting gold to create an idol of a calf for the people to worship. The choice of a cow should not be surprising, for it is from cattle that the people received milk to drink, meat to eat, transportation, and leather that could be worked into tents and clothing. God might be a war god, the people concluded, but food, nourishment, and shelter came from another source. Thus, the calf served as the focal point to worship a fertility deity. When Moses saw what Aaron and the others had done, he became furious, threw down the stone tablets in anger and broke them, and ordered the calf to be destroyed.

32

Despite this injunction, despite Moses' close connection with God, within a very short time Moses violated this commandment. In Numbers, chapter 21, we read that for a period the Israelites were plagued by snakes, and many were dying from their bites. Moses had his metalworkers cast a bronze snake and place it on a post so those who were bitten could look on it and be instantly cured. Though the snake was to remind the people of God's power, all too soon it was interpreted as being a god, and Moses discontinued its use.

Throughout the long history of Israel, a constant spiritual war was waged against idolatry and the violation of the other commandments. In the Book of Judges, we read how the rulers were judged solely on their zeal and faithfulness to God. In the history texts (i.e., Chronicles and 1 and 2 Kings), "good" kings pulled down the ashrams and high places and mandated a keeping of the Sabbath; "wicked" kings allowed the people to worship at these pagan shrines and were tolerant of idolatry.

This leaves Christians wondering how scrupulously they must obey this commandment. On the one hand, Jesus said that he had come to fulfill the law and the prophets, and that to disobey any of the commandments, much less teach others to be disobedient, was a grave sin. On the other hand, as Christians we affirm that we now live under a new covenant, and that some of the old laws no longer apply to us. But are we to burn all our photographs, put a knife through our most treasured paintings, break all our stained-glass windows, destroy all our statues, and paint over all our murals? Some of the more conservative groups within other religions (primarily within Judaism and Islam) would say yes. And indeed Christians through the ages have agreed, and have beheaded statues and destroyed all manner of church ornamentation. The more fundamentalist Muslim sects, renowned for their beautiful geometric designs and intricate mosaics, are diametrically opposed to any physical representation of a living being. Somewhat more liberal Muslim groups carefully white out the face of Mohammed, believing him to be such a holy man that it is wrong to show his face. When the Muslims conquered Greece during the late Middle Ages, they whitewashed all the mosaics and frescoes on chapel walls in monasteries and parish churches. Only now, more than 140 years after gaining their independence, are some of the Greek churches fully restored. Similarly, the more conservative and orthodox Jews are so careful about obeying this commandment that they will write God's name as "G-d" rather than spell it out.

Some Christian groups also take this injunction seriously. Small denominations and sects such as the Hutterites, the Mennonites, and the Old Order Amish also forbid photographs or paintings of people or animals. And the Doukhobors, a small sect of ultraconservative Russian and Ukrainian Christians now living in western Canada, have taken it even further. Periodically they choose to burn their barns or strip off their clothing and process naked through their small farming communities as a demonstration that they will not allow the created and material things to ever supplant the Creator.

G. Corwin Stoppel

For Episcopalians, obedience to this commandment is a greater challenge than we might at first imagine. We are part of a long denominational history dating back to the time of King Henry VIII of England, and even further back to the founding of the Church itself. Our history is rich with colorful characters, eminent leaders in all areas of life, a vital and ever-expanding ethos, and at the same time, a great reverence for our traditions. Despite all our differences, whether we are high, low, broad, or charismatic churchmen and churchwomen, we are bound together by our use of the *Book of Common Prayer.* With good reason, many of us believe it is the finest and most formal liturgical worship ever created for the proper worship of God. And therein is the danger: We can become so attached to the prayer book, our liturgy and traditions, and our reverence for the past that they become our new idols.

The potential for idolatry within the Episcopal Church seems to come at us from all directions. When I was first ordained, the "new" 1976 *Book of Common Prayer* had been in use for only a few years. Women had been ordained for only a decade, and it would be several more years before the first woman would be consecrated as a bishop. Although many welcomed the new liturgical language and the expanded role of women, many utterly detested it. For them, the 1928 *Book of Common Prayer* was the only appropriate form of worship, and women had no place behind the altar rail. The denomination as a whole was divided over it, as were many parishes. Some members and parishes left to form new denominations; others banded together under the auspices of the Evangelical Catholic Movement or the Prayer Book Society in an attempt to bring back past traditions. Only a handful of older members, most of them now deceased, remembered that in the late 1920s, they had had the same dispute when the liturgy from the 1860s was replaced by what was then the "new" (1928) *Book of Common Prayer.*

Therein lies the challenge: Are we worshipping God through Jesus Christ, or have we Anglicans and Episcopalians made our traditions into idols? Are we open to the new, or are we trying to keep God in a box of our own making by clinging to the past? How far can we go in maintaining our ethos and our forms of worship without losing what we value? Those questions do not have any simple answers. Nor can they be answered with a blanket statement or hard-and-fast rules. Rather, each individual must search his or her own soul to determine if he or she is worshipping the Creator or the created. Legislation, canons, rules, and wholesale destruction will not work. Nor will running away. It is an individual matter of discernment and intentional choice on how we will live.

Fortunately, we have a model in Jesus for making those decisions. The Gospels tell the story of the rich young man (in some instances, the rich young ruler) who sought to become a disciple. He assured Jesus that he had scrupulously obeyed the commandments since childhood, and then wanted to know what more he needed to do to find spiritual fulfillment and attain salvation. Knowing that he was a wealthy man, Jesus told him to first give away all that he had to the poor; then he could become a disciple. The Gospels report that the man turned away in sorrow because he was unwilling to part with his wealth.

Jesus was not opposed to wealth and money, but rather to the damage those and other possessions could do to one's spiritual growth. In this case, the young man's money was more important to him than his relationship with God. It had effectively become an idol. He had made his wealth into his security blanket—trusting in gold and silver instead of God. Therein lies the heart of the problem with idolatry.

Idols not only come between God and ourselves and interrupt our relationship, but also become our safety net and security blanket. They are a poor substitute for the safety and security offered to us in God through Jesus Christ, yet we embrace them because they are immediate and tangible.

Christian maturity means moving away from childishly clutching a security blanket of our own making to putting our faith and trust in the living God.

✦

CHAPTER THREE

So Help Me, God

THE THIRD COMMANDMENT

*Thou shall not take the name of the
Lord your God in vain.*

HAD AN UNCLE who could have taken first-class honors in any swearing contest in the world. The more angry and frustrated he became, the louder, longer, and more convoluted and profane his oaths. In a single sentence, he could invoke the names of the Trinity, the Holy Family, at least half the Apostles, and even some of the more obscure saints. He was an absolute wonder to behold, particularly because in our immediate family, even the phrase "gosh darn" was forbidden as being a tad too close to shattering the third commandment. Once, when I dared to imitate him, I paid the penalty of standing in the bathroom for a full ten minutes with a bar of Ivory soap in my mouth as Mother lectured me that God's last name was not "Damn." I quickly learned that it was far safer to blow off a little verbal steam with the more creative expletive "Balsam Juice!" No one else knew where it came from (from my favorite writer, Sam Campbell) or what it meant (absolutely nothing!), and the mystery alone made it sound all the more risqué and dangerous.

There are three basic reasons we use expletives. The first is to add emphasis, passion, or shock value to a statement. For example, if we hit our thumb with a hammer, we may break forth with a loud curse and some jumping around to let everyone within hearing range know that we are hurting. Muttering a quiet "Oh my, that really is an owie," doesn't quite cut it. Yet, in reality, neither a quiet comment nor a blast of profanity has any actual impact on reducing our pain, and if we so desired, we could train ourselves to suffer in silence. Indeed, this is what is taught in some martial arts courses and among some religious groups where a high emphasis is placed on self-discipline and self-control.

The second reason is closely related: Swearing calls attention to ourselves. If we hit our thumb with a hammer and start swearing, we let everyone know that we are hurting. Whether they laugh at our clumsiness or empathize with us, we have succeeded in letting them know that we are suffering. Even if we are not hurting, we may use expletives to call attention to ourselves, to prove that we are full-fledged members of our peer group, or to make a reputation for ourselves. Once the almost exclusive province of men, the practice of swearing has been picked up by many women in our more egalitarian society, if for no other reason than to assert their equality with men. We have also witnessed many contemporary musicians and entertainers who have intentionally incorporated "filthy language" into their routines as a means of establishing their reputation or shocking their audiences. One of the first to do this was the late Lenny Bruce, who, throughout his comedic career, took pride in being arrested for his shocking language and his ability to draw attention to himself. Recently, the Supreme Court and many state and lower courts have decreed that although profane expletives are shocking to polite and conventional society, they must be tolerated under the First Amendment to the Constitution, which guarantees freedom of speech.

The problem with using expletives for emphasis or as a means of drawing attention to ourselves is that after a relatively short time, they begin to lose their impact. When the word *darn* becomes commonplace, then it must be escalated to *damn*, and when *damn* is no longer sufficient for shock value, additional adjectives must be used. A quick review of the language used on radio and television or in films over the past century shows that the words that once

38

incurred the wrath of the censors are now commonplace. In 1939, when Rhett Butler said "damn" in the movie *Gone with the Wind*, clergy, censors, and arbiters of polite society were united in their indignation. Now the word scarcely raises an eyebrow. Perhaps one of the best-known moments of television censorship came in the 1960s, when the late-night talk show host Jack Paar walked off the stage and quit as the host of the *Tonight Show* because censors would not allow him to use the initials "W.C.," standing for water closet, or toilet. Even though several weeks later the dispute was resolved and Paar returned to the program, today such censorship seems laughable.

The third reason people use expletives is their lack of an adequate vocabulary. To some this may seem like an elitist observation, but I make no apology for it because reality bears out its truth. Often those who are not able to adequately express their emotions, who have a need for filling in the "blank air" of a conversation, or who have learned by habit to use such words resort to base and crude language.

Therefore, in light of our culture's tolerance for almost any form of language, we would do well if we remembered nothing more about this commandment than "God's last name is not 'Damn.'" Yet, there is more to this law than the prohibition against using an expletive. In exploring it further, we learn more about ourselves, about what Christ requires of us, and about the nature of God.

39

The key phrase in this commandment is "in vain." First, *vanity* means "unreality." A vain person, for example, is someone who cannot or will not face reality. They are a marketer's dream! Daily we are bombarded by advertisements that promote products to make us appear thinner, appear stronger, smell better, look better, be more virile, or appear younger, wealthier, smarter, or better connected than anyone else. We can spend billions of dollars every year on these products, not because we actually need them, nor because they live up to their statements, but because we are persuaded that we must have them if we are going to "fit in" or set the standard for others to follow. So, people line up to buy a diploma from a mail-order school because they were not able to go to college or graduate school; they purchase spray-on hair (actually cheap spray paint) to cover bald spots; or they go to the "right" vacation spots to demonstrate their achievement, status, and sophistication to the rest of the world. Individuals pad their resumes, have books ghostwritten on their behalf, and even buy titles from impoverished nobility. However it is expressed or acted on, vanity is sheer deception. We attempt to deceive others by promoting ourselves as something we are not, and we live in fear that sooner or later the reality will be discovered. As in the tale of the Emperor's new clothes, ultimately we are deceiving only ourselves.

Anyone who is drawn into this lifestyle soon finds it difficult to escape. We have all encountered or heard of tragic individuals who were fairly affluent and influential—until something happened. Perhaps their spouse deserted them or died, their finances turned sour, or they lost their job, retired, or were demoted. Rather than face the reality of their new situation, they pretend that nothing is wrong. They continue to spend money they don't have, and pretend that everything is as it has been in the past. Others may see through their vanity but say nothing, leaving them to think they have succeeded. Unless challenged, in time they may come to believe that their vanity is their reality. Such people are to be pitied more than condemned, and fortunate if they have a friend or loved one who will provide a much-needed "reality check."

Other synonyms for *vain* include futile, useless, hopeless, meaningless, and helpless. The Old Testament Book of Ecclesiastes offers another clear picture of how God interprets this type of vanity. The first and second chapters are a lengthy recitation of how everything, from work to the accumulation of wealth to living a luxurious life of leisure, is all in vain. None of those things bring the happiness the anonymous writer had anticipated. None of them are fulfilling, useful, or joyous, despite all their glittering promises. It is all meaningless, and at the end of the day, the writer realized he had no hope for a brighter future, and that life itself is vain.

The same concept is reflected throughout the New Testament. Paul wrote that if Jesus did not die on the cross and was not resurrected from the dead, then all our hopes for eternal life are in vain, we have been deceived, and we are the most pitiful of all creatures. He also teaches in many of his writings that life without a relationship with Jesus is in vain, and that trying to fulfill all the laws of the Old Testament to earn one's way into heaven is a useless effort. He tells us there is great value in receiving Communion, but unless we first examine our souls, we receive the body and blood of Christ to the detriment of our souls.

Conversely, in the Epistle of James, we are warned that faith without works is meaningless (i.e., vain), but so also is work without faith in Jesus as the savior. He asks what good it is to talk about faith to a person who is destitute. Rather, we should look after physical needs as well as share the Good News of Jesus Christ. It is wrong and pure vanity to extend a warm welcome to a wealthy person while marginalizing and excluding the poor. It is vanity to believe that material things will ensure our entrance into heaven.

41

Throughout the centuries many Christians have embraced the teachings of Paul and rejected James's concept of works and faith. Indeed, Martin Luther attempted to excise the Epistle of James from the Bible—in vain, I hasten to add! For those who believe that faith in Jesus Christ is sufficient for salvation, rejection of the Epistle of James seems quite natural. As we consider the wider implications of this commandment, this letter reminds us that there are many different kinds of vanity.

Though these days we usually think of oaths as the kind of expletives my flamboyant uncle utters—oftentimes incorporating a religious reference—the biblical understanding and intention of oaths is very different. Typically it is a solemn promise to perform a task, or an equally solemn promise not to do something. We see an abundance of oaths in the Bible, especially in the Old Testament.

Perhaps one of the earliest and best-known promises from God came as the Great Flood ended. God painted a rainbow in the sky and promised that never again would the earth be destroyed by a flood. Later, when Jerusalem was besieged by Nebuchadnezzar and the entire Babylonian army, God, through Isaiah and Jeremiah, promised the restoration of Israel and the coming of a messiah who would rescue the Israelites.

We also see a number of solemn human promises. When Joshua and Aaron were about to lead the people across the Jordan River and back into the Promised Land, their leaders assembled the people before them and asked them if they were committed to obeying the laws of God or not. They gave their assent, although we soon read that they do not completely fulfill their part of the agreement. In the story of young David during the reign of King Saul, we see David keeping inviolate his promise of loyalty; even when Saul turned against him and forced him to become an outlaw, David would not take his life. We also find, only a matter of hours before Saul and his son Jonathan are killed in battle, Jonathan and David pledging to remain friends despite the dangers they face, including Saul's desire to kill David. Then, several hundred years later, as God fulfills his promise to restore the people back to Jerusalem, Ezra and Nehemiah assemble all the people before the Water Gate to read and explain and law and the prophets, and to ask for their consent in the imposition of the laws. Just as in the story of Joshua and Aaron, the people make promises they are not quite able to fulfill. In many of the Old Testament stories where a promise is made, it is signified by building a rustic stone altar, or even a cairn, as a reminder or a witness of the solemnity of the day and what had been said there.

42

In the New Testament, we need only one example: Jesus. His promises of coming back to life after three days, of being the way back home to God, and of being the Son of God are sufficient. Unlike the Old Testament where signs and tangible items are used to prove the validity and solemnity of the promises, Jesus' words stand alone.

Such promises may be either explicit or implicit, and are sometimes subject to interpretation. We may not realize we are making or receiving an oath, simply because it happens on such a routine basis. Such instances happen in both the secular and the spiritual side of life.

For example, whenever an elected official is inaugurated, there is a "swearing in" ceremony, during which the individual takes the oath of office. When President Washington took his oath of office, he solemnly promised to uphold the Constitution and to fulfill his duties as chief executive. Then, suddenly realizing the significance of his responsibilities, he spontaneously added the words, "So help me, God," and leaned down to kiss the Bible. Even though it is not required by law, every president since that time has imitated him.

We also give or receive formal oaths of office from many nongovernment employees, professionals, and volunteers. On passing the bar examination, new lawyers take a specific oath, and newly licensed physicians take the Hippocratic oath, which dates back to the ancient Greeks. When a young person joins the Boy Scouts or the Girl Scouts, one of the first things they must commit to memory is the Scout oath. Whenever they step out of line, their leaders and peers are quick to remind them of their promises. In the Episcopal Church, at their ordination or at the Celebration of a New Ministry service, clergy make solemn promises before their bishop, parishioners, and others who have come to witness or participate in the service that they will fulfill their responsibilities.

◆
43

We are making an oath every time we make a financial transaction, promising to the individual or business to whom we are giving a check or a credit card that we have sufficient money in our account to make good our purchases. The same principle applies when we take out a mortgage, buy insurance, borrow money from a bank, or make any other transfer of goods and services. On trading floors or at auctions, a wave of the hand, a flick of the finger, or a handshake is deemed to be an inviolable oath. Those who betray their promises are rarely trusted again.

Unfortunately, at times individuals or corporations have not fulfilled their explicit and implicit oaths. In the nineteenth century, meat-packing factories and pharmaceutical companies often grossly misstated the contents and purity of their products, causing the deaths of thousands of people. Railroads, which had the implicit trust of transporting goods and people, so violated the principles by which they were organized that the federal government was forced to take action to regulate these and other industries.

As individuals we often make implicit promises to one another. For couples it might be a tradition establishing Friday night as their "date night" and that they are going to preserve that time to do something together. It causes great hurt and tension when one partner selfishly decides to do something on her or his own or with other friends on that particular night. We tell a person, "I'll be home early," without defining what time "early" might be, yet we imply it will not be worrisomely late, or we will telephone to explain our delay. The violation of these and other implicit promises can create as much tension in a relationship as the violation of an explicit vow.

No matters who breaks the oath, the results are always the same—an intentional betrayal of trust, an attempt to do something we instinctively know to be wrong or at least uncaring and unmindful of others, and the disappointment felt by those affected by such unfortunate actions.

◆

44

In our spiritual lives, we give and receive many oaths under the auspices of the Church—marriage, baptism, Confirmation, and even receiving Communion. For example, when a couple comes to a clergyperson for premarital counseling, together they explore the meaning of their wedding vows. The very fact that they are coming to a church for a Christian marriage service means they intend to live up to their promises before God, their families, and the wider Christian community. They discuss what it means to love, honor, and remain faithful to each other. Then, on their wedding day, they say their vows with a full understanding of what they are pledging. It is always a great tragedy for everyone when one or both partners do not honor the vows they made, but it is far worse—a violation of this commandment—when they make the vows without intending to keep them.

At baptism specific vows are given and received by the parents and godparents on behalf of the child (or by the individual if he or she is old enough to make the vows on his or her own behalf), the congregation, and before God. Not all parents and godparents who have a child baptized understand the importance of the vows; they often see the day as more of a social event where they can draw the entire family and many friends together for a party.

The liturgy of this sacrament requires specific vows from all the participants, and must be taken seriously if they are to have any genuine meaning in our Christian formation. We soon come to realize that not only is the fulfillment of the vows our life's work and vocation as Christians, but also that they are seemingly impossible to accomplish. For example, we promise to uphold the dignity of every human and yet find it difficult to do when we are angry, frustrated, or frightened. At times we may not even be aware that what we are doing demeans or harms another person. Or, we promise to reject the works of Satan. We can give mental and spiritual agreement to that concept, but when it comes to putting it into practice, we are not always certain what are the works of Satan.

As a congregation we promise to support and uphold the parents and godparents in the spiritual raising of their child. Yet, we adults who make those promises can be the very ones who don't want children to participate in worship or are opposed to increasing the budget to underwrite the costs of expanding the Sunday school. We neglect to make the telephone calls or visits to parents who haven't been in church, or to offer to do whatever we can to assist them in raising their child. We are often quick to criticize the mistakes of a young acolyte or to find fault when a youngster brings a teddy bear to the communion rail and holds it up to receive a blessing. As a congregation we are sometimes more concerned about the formality of our worship service or the beauty of our building than with making it an inviting experience for a newcomer.

At Confirmation young people and adults again make specific promises—to give their wholehearted affirmation to all the vows made by their parents and godparents at their baptism, and to be supportive of the work and life of the Church. But many congregations come to realize that the Sunday of Confirmation is all too often the last Sunday for many years that a teenager is in church. The teens are not fulfilling their promises, and neither are we who promised to provide a place at the table for them. Youth are quick to recognize the incongruity that at Confirmation they are considered to be adult members of the parish, yet are often deemed too young, too immature, or too inexperienced to serve on a church committee.

As we carefully and prayerfully study the vows we make in the sacraments and rites of the Church, we come to realize the great potential for breaking or not fulfilling them. Indeed, they are almost impossible for us to keep. Does this mean that we should not make these or any other vows because we might not be able to do everything we promised? Of course not! Rather, we should approach these solemn and sacred vows determining whether we intend to do our best to fulfill our promises. John Wesley taught wisely when he said that we are not perfect people, but are going on to perfection! And we do so with God's help, with God's grace.

So it is not only wrong to make a vow, secular or sacred, when we have no intention of keeping it in the first place, or when we have not given serious thought as to how we will fulfill it. It is the individual writing a check knowing there is no money in the account and not the person who makes an honest mathematical mistake who is wrong. It is the man or woman entering into marriage with no intention of being faithful to his or her partner who is violating this commandment. It is the parents who are more interested in the parish reception or the family celebration after a baptism than in making a good-faith attempt to do all they promised who sin. That is the vanity against which this commandment speaks.

Vows are also empty and vain when the person or group receiving them holds them in such low esteem that they treat them with contempt or make no effort to hold the person accountable for keeping her or his word. Cheapening the value of a vow in this fashion is as dishonest as the maker not trying to fulfill it. For whenever we make a promise or a vow, we are literally giving our word and staking our personal reputation that we will do what we promise. Perhaps the highest accolade a person can earn is that of being someone who can be trusted to keep promises.

We now see the two elements come together: the promise and the need to emphasize the significance of a vow by invoking the name of God. Because we deem certain promises so extraordinarily important, merely giving our word in our own name does not seem sufficient. Therefore, we add the words, "So help me, God," or "As God is my witness." Certainly, these additional phrases magnify the solemnity and sincerity of our vows, but it is not only our words or intentions that count. We mere mortals have now brought God into the picture.

So, this third commandment does not teach against giving or receiving an oath in the name of God. After all, we make such promises all the time in church. Rather, it teaches: "If you are going to break your word and lie, if you have no intention of keeping the promises you are making, then do not bring my name into it. My name is holy, and I will have no part of your deception."

When Jesus was asked about the meaning of this commandment, he cut to the heart of the matter. He said we should not swear at all. Don't give or take any vows. Don't invoke any power greater than yourself to emphasize your intention. Rather, live such a blameless and upright life, establish such a good reputation that "Your yes is your yes and your no is your no." In short, Jesus was telling his listeners to be people of their word.

It is human nature to seek a loophole, and many of our Lord's contemporaries believed they had found one. They scrupulously would never take an oath in the name of God, and, as we noted earlier, were so careful to maintain the sanctity of his name that they would spell it "G-d." However, they would invoke the power of heaven, earth, Jerusalem, or anything else in their vows. In today's language we might say, "I swear on my mother's grave," or some similar phrase.

Like most loopholes it has the appearance of legitimacy, but it is a false one. Everything imaginable, even life itself—including the hairs on our head, according to Jesus—is

◆

47

from the hand of God. So, even though we may not use the precise words invoking the name of God in our oaths, God is still incorporated into it by virtue of everything being sacred. The only logical recourse is to follow the simple instruction offered by Jesus of having such a sterling reputation for honesty that our yes is sufficient.

There is another pernicious way of violating this commandment: doing something wicked and then justifying our actions by claiming that it is God's will or that we are speaking on God's behalf when, in reality, it is our own agenda we are proposing. We see numerous examples of this both in the Old and the New Testaments and in contemporary life.

During the monarchy of the Old Testament era, from the time of King Saul until the destruction of Jerusalem by the Babylonians, there were many prophets throughout Israel. Basically they fell into two categories—true prophets and false prophets. The true prophets, often highly unpopular, hated, persecuted, and sometimes even tortured and killed because of their messages, had the courage to speak the true word of God to the people. For example, we find Amos courageously warning that the unrighteous and wicked behavior of the people would bring about judgment on the entire nation. Jeremiah, also giving a stern warning to the people, was cast into a well; Isaiah was very likely killed by the rulers he served. All the prophets of the Old Testament suffered at the hands of those who did not like what they were hearing.

Conversely, the false prophets were often under the protection of the king or queen and, for the most part, told the rulers and the people the comforting messages they wanted to hear. In today's business language, we would derisively call them "yes men." They rarely challenged anyone and kept assuring the people that they were divinely blessed because they were descendants of Abraham. If the king wanted to go to war, the false prophets would assure him that he was doing God's will and would win. If he wanted to raise taxes, abuse the poor, or harm the foreign sojourner, the false prophets would say it was acceptable. If the ruler wanted to allow or encourage the worship of false deities and idols, the prophets would assure him that it was quite all right and that strict obedience to the Mosaic laws was passé. If the true prophets spoke out against the public policies of the rulers, the false prophets would pronounce that the ruler was on his throne because God had placed him there, and therefore he could do no wrong. In short, the false prophets claimed to be speaking on behalf of God when, in reality, they were not.

In the Gospels we find the most blatant of all examples of falsely using the name of God to accomplish a wicked action. Jesus had become a thorn in the side of the religious establishment for many years, and finally the chief priests and other temple authorities were able to arrest him. Because only the Romans could impose a death sentence, they took Jesus to Pontius Pilate and made their accusations before him. At first Pilate was unimpressed. Israel, he told them, was a country full of religious fanatics and prophets, and he took Jesus to be just another one of many such men. Only when the religious leaders convinced him that Jesus was an insurrectionist and a threat to public safety and that his message was so upsetting the people that it threatened the stability of the government did Pilate order the death sentence. The temple leadership and those who sympathized with them believed they were doing God's will by ridding the country of a blasphemer, a troublemaker, and a rebel leader—even though they had lied to accomplish their goals.

49

This theme recurs in the Epistles with the story of Simeon, who wanted to buy his way into a leadership role in the Church, and again in some of the snippets of Paul's constant battles with the gnostic Christians, who, according to many of his letters, were attempting to pervert the Gospel message with a heretical version of their own.

Tragically, the history of the Christian Church is filled with examples of military campaigns, wars, and persecutions of all types being done in the name of God. For a time King Henry II of England believed he was doing God's work when he ordered the murder of Archbishop of Canterbury Thomas Becket. When the Crusaders broke through the walls of Jerusalem in 1099, they began a wholesale slaughter of combatants and civilians—Muslim, Jew, and Christian alike—believing they were doing God's will. One commander went so far as to order the massacre to continue, solemnly pronouncing that "God will know his own," implying that murdered Christians would gain immediate entrance into heaven while all others would be consigned to hell. When wars broke out between the Protestants and the Roman Catholics during the Reformation and the Counter-Reformation, during the Spanish Inquisition, and during the persecution of the Moors and Jews in Spain, they were always justified in the minds of the offenders by the claim that they were done according to the will of God.

Similarly, we have enslaved Africans and others, built our great industries on the backs of underpaid and unprotected laborers, repressed women and minorities, justified child labor, violated the civil rights of many innocent people, suppressed knowledge and vital supplies to others, and destroyed many freedoms—all under the guise of protecting the Christian Church and "our way of life." Yet, at the same time, people from other religions and nations whom we label terrorists claim that what they are doing is justified in the name of their deity.

Wherever this happens it is blasphemy and a total violation of this commandment because it is far removed from the message of peace and love exemplified by Jesus Christ.

This commandment calls us to live truly integrated and honest lives in which we have no need to use any oath. We are to establish, from childhood on, a personal reputation for being straightforward in both our actions and our words. We are never permitted to do our own will by falsely claiming that it is commanded by God or that we are acting in God's name. True obedience to this commandment is a matter of moving ever closer to God's will for us and for God's world.

CHAPTER FOUR

✦

Weekly Refreshment for Body and Soul

THE FOURTH COMMANDMENT

You shall keep holy the Sabbath day.

IMAGINE ISSUING A TICKET to the commander in chief of the United States! That's what happened to George Washington one day in Connecticut. The charge? He was taking a pleasure ride on his horse on a Sunday afternoon, for which he was fined five dollars. Such was the prevailing belief in maintaining the sanctity of the Sabbath, according to that state's Blue Laws.

Even today, when most malls and many stores are open for business, many people feel uncomfortable shopping on Sunday. Still others question whether it is right to mow their lawn or work in the garden, go out for Sunday lunch after church, or engage in any type of recreation— including watching television. Not far from where I live in Saugatuck, Michigan, some communities still have local ordinances that forbid businesses to be open or regulate what merchandise can be sold on Sunday. So how did this special treatment of Sunday, or the Sabbath, come about?

There is nothing unique to the Jews about a seven-day week. Many of the ancient Middle East cultures, as well as civilizations elsewhere in the world, had already worked out a calendar based on that model. The reason for it is simple: Astronomers and astrologers had determined that there were seven days between each phase of the moon, and in time, the number of days in the months was finally established as we know them today.

What was unique to the ancient Jews was dividing the week into six days of work and one day of rest. Other civilizations also had divided their weeks into days of labor and rest, adding the occasional special day for religious or secular observances, but none to the extent and dedication of the Jews, for whom this break from work became a sacred act of worship. Their model for this was God, who took a day of rest after creating the universe in six "days." Six days a week were sufficient for work; on the seventh day, all labor was to cease. Quite literally, what was good for God was good for God's people, and the mandated day of rest helped keep them connected with the Creator.

There is a good, rational reason for this division of labor and rest: Endless work is destructive to mind and body. We need time for recreation and re-creation. Efficiency experts have come to realize that ceaseless work quickly becomes counterproductive. In numerous studies, those who have become so addicted to work that they can be diagnosed as workaholics experience a greater incidence of chemical abuse, have higher divorce rates, have shorter life spans, and often suffer more serious mental problems than those who lead a balanced life. Even the military, not always known for its sensitive consideration of human life, has learned the importance of taking soldiers out of combat or active duty for rest and recreation behind the front lines or off the base.

52

In an ideal culture or society, we would embrace the basic human need for rest, but we often we do not have the wisdom to do what is best for us and for those around us. Beginning early in the twentieth century in the United States, the federal government, using its powers to regulate interstate commerce, established minimum-wage laws, created the Pure Food and Drug Administration, established numerous federal wildlife preserves, and enacted other laws for the benefit of all people. President Theodore Roosevelt's rationale was simple: If industry and business were not willing to do the right thing by the people, the government would intervene.

The fourth commandment likewise attempts to prevent abuse of self and others by mandating a day of rest. In the case of ancient Israel, it was a day of rest not only for free Jewish men and women, but for their children, their slaves, their livestock, and even for foreign travelers or residents in their land. Out of concern for all people and all creation, God made provision for all creation's well-being.

What would life be like with a mandated day of rest? Stores would not be open, nor would restaurants—giving employees a day off to be with their families. We would not be bombarded by thick Sunday newspapers, and we would not feel compelled to go into the office to catch up on undone work from the previous week nor to get a head start on the tasks for the following day. Certainly it would be a radical shift in the way many Americans live. But would this be a genuine hardship, a mere inconvenience, or a radical but welcome adjustment to our lives?

Like the other commandments, this one lays down the basic precept, but then leaves its application up to the individual or the community. For theologians, philosophers, and seekers of knowledge, the first challenge was to define the nature of work. At first, that seems simple enough, but for the religious leaders from the time of Moses through the Pharisees of our Lord's era and on to the rabbis of our own age, it was far more complicated. In the Talmud (the commentaries on the Torah) are transcripts of lengthy debates as to the nature of work and how one could be more obedient to this commandment.

Take the debate about nails. Obviously, erecting a house or building a cabinet would be construed as work, and to do it on the Sabbath would be a violation of this commandment. Therefore, construction and shop work did not occur. Even carrying nails about on a construction site or in the woodworker's shop constitutes work. But, a scholar asked, what if the carpenter did not realize that he had overlooked a nail in his pocket. Does his inadvertent carrying of the nail constitute work? And because small nails or brads were often used to hold together sandals, if a man or a woman wore sandals that contained nails on the Sabbath, was that a violation of the law?

Or take the debate about lighting a fire, whether for warmth, for cooking, or for illumination. Does that constitute work? Because the Sabbath begins at sundown on Friday evening, all work to do with fires for that day and the next would have to be completed before sundown: Meals would have to be prepared, not only for that evening but for the following day; fires would have to be laid and lit; and lamps would need to be filled with sufficient oil and their wicks trimmed so that they would last for twenty-four hours—for even to light, trim, or refill a lamp—would constitute work. And finally, the house would be tidied and cleaned and, whenever possible, each individual would bathe and ritually prepare for the Sabbath.

Our modern technology has added new challenges to obeying this law. For example, the injunction against performing work on the Sabbath must now be expanded to take into consideration such things as elevators, electric lights, and other appliances. Today, in many modern hotels in Israel and elsewhere, elevators are designed with specific settings for the Sabbath, whereby they automatically open on the main floor, close before going directly to the top floor, and stop at each floor on the way down. That way Orthodox Jews do not have to violate the Sabbath by performing the work of pushing buttons. In some instances it is possible to be escorted by a nonpracticing Jew or a non-Jew who will unlock the room door and turn on the lights. In other cases, once guests are in their rooms, motion detectors automatically turn on the lights, and then shut them off if there is no activity after a certain amount of time.

Still another form of work was to travel from one place to another. Land transportation in biblical times meant traveling either by foot or by animal power, and because animals were included in this commandment of rest, walking or riding from one place to another was forbidden. Because it was irrational to make everyone remain perfectly immobile on the Sabbath, eventually scholars concluded that one could travel a "Sabbath's Day journey," or about a quarter of a mile, without violating the law. That allowed people to move about freely in their house, perhaps to visit close neighbors, and most important, to worship and study together. This became all the more important in the centuries following the Babylonian Exile and the Diaspora, when the Jews were forced from their native land. Today, in some predominantly Orthodox neighborhoods in this country, a colored wire is strung through the trees and light poles, defining the distance the residents can travel and still remain within the letter of the law.

As these illustrations demonstrate, the rabbis, scholars, and people sincerely wanted to obey this commandment, and their hearts were, at least initially, in the right place. But as they tried to discern what was right or wrong and make a rule for every possible contingency, they often became legalistic and petty. Their laws became increasingly complex and convoluted, sometimes contradictory, and so frustrating that they began to alienate people from one another and from their spiritual leaders. When that happened people began to lose sight of the original intent and meaning of the Sabbath. Instead of a day of rest and an opportunity to reflect on the goodness and bounty of God, the Sabbath became a day on which it was a considerable challenge to do all the right things.

55

Indeed, from the time of the Judges through the following centuries, on many occasions the Sabbath was not observed. The authors of the history books (i.e., Judges, 1 and 2 Kings, 1 and 2 Chronicles) note that some rulers did not impose a strict observance of the Sabbath on their people, and were therefore deemed to be wicked men. Others revived the Sabbath observances and enforced the day of rest and worship, and were deemed to be good judges or kings.

One of the frequent criticisms of Jesus by the Pharisees, scribes, and other opponents was that he violated the Sabbath by healing the sick, teaching, or engaging in other forms of "work" on that day. For example, when Jesus healed the man who had suffered from some form of paralysis for thirty-nine years, the Pharisees were quick to complain that he had violated this commandment. One can see their point. After all, the man had been suffering from the illness for almost his entire life, and one more day would not have made a difference. But Jesus was attempting to teach a more important lesson and restore the original meaning of the fourth commandment: The Sabbath was made for man, not man for the Sabbath. In other words, this one day of rest each week was a blessing, a gift, from God, to be wisely used for good purposes. It was not intended to be an exercise in scrupulous obedience to a number of man-made rules.

It is interesting that this commandment assumes work but not pleasure to be an essential part of life. The Sabbath was a day of rest from work. It did not mean that people could not enjoy themselves—they ate and spent time together having fun, talking, and relaxing. It is the more conservative Reformed-Calvinist tradition within Christianity that tries to limit the more fun and recreational aspects of the day. Case in point: Some miles from here is a little Dutch Reformed Community where merely sitting on one's front porch and drinking a beer on Sunday afternoon is sufficient cause for a neighbor to call the police and file a complaint. This is a Calvinist interpretation, not Jewish: It is work that is proscribed, not pleasure. Somewhere in the Talmud is the instruction that the Sabbath is a pretty darned good day for a husband and wife to "know" each other. Want to bet those Calvinists don't interpret it that way?

◆
56

The Sabbath observance, as noted above, formally began at sunset on Friday, at which time all work ceased. In a traditional household, the family would gather together for what was usually their best meal of the week, presided over by the senior woman of the household. Sometimes other family members, neighbors, or nearby friends might be invited to share the meal and the evening. After the blessing of the food and the breaking of bread, the family enjoyed their meal together. The following day included opportunities for long conversations, for study of the Scriptures and debates over its meanings and interpretations, and for play. The Sabbath concluded at sunset on Saturday, and on Sunday morning, work resumed.

Today Jews observe the Sabbath in a variety of ways. Just as for nominal Christians, for some Jews, especially those who consider themselves to be "cultural" (i.e., nonobservant or nonpracticing) Jews, this day means very little in religious terms. For them it represents a day off from work and a good meal; they are quite content to miss worship at their synagogue or temple and pay little attention to the traditional rules. For others it is a day of rest and relaxation. For the more orthodox observers, it is a day whose rules are still strictly enforced.

Obedience to the Sabbath laws plays a pivotal role in the Passion narratives of Jesus and the history of the Christian Church. Jesus was sentenced to death and crucified on Friday, the day of preparation for the Sabbath. Because it was against Jewish law for a body to remain unburied over the Sabbath—all the more so when it was the Passover Sabbath!—Pontius Pilate gave permission for Joseph of Arimathea and a few others to take Jesus' body down from the cross. They hastily did the preliminary preparations for burial, then laid his body in the tomb. There Jesus' body remained for all of Saturday (i.e., the Sabbath) in rest, and he arose on the first day of the Jewish week, Sunday. Because of the Sabbath laws, none of his followers traveled to the tomb until Sunday morning. They had come to complete the burial preparations, but to their shock and surprise, the stone had been rolled away and the tomb was empty. Only later, when the women and the disciples realized that his body had not been stolen, and that he was not dead but resurrected, did they begin celebrating this joyous occasion each Sunday. For them Sunday, rather than Saturday, became "the Lord's Day." With the exception of several small Christian sects, in particular the Seventh-Day Adventists, to this day Christians proclaim Sunday as their holy day, while Jews still retain Saturday as their Sabbath.

For the first years, those earliest Jewish Christians maintained their identity as Jews, seeing themselves more as members of a new and nontraditional sect or group within Judaism (much like the Pharisees, Sadducees, Essenes, and

◆

others) rather than as members of an entirely new religion. From Acts of the Apostles and some of Paul's earliest letters, along with numerous noncanonical books, it is clear that they continued to worship at the Temple in Jerusalem or in synagogues throughout Israel and other parts of the Roman Empire. Likewise, they continued to observe all the ancient Jewish traditions and holy days and remained obedient to many of the laws. We read of the Apostles preaching on the plaza in front of the Temple and of Paul and his companions going to the synagogues to teach the message of Jesus as the Christ and the long-awaited Messiah.

That should not be surprising to us. After all, Jesus was born, raised, lived, and died as a Jew. Paul took pride in the fact that he had been the foremost of all the Pharisees (surely, something of a hyperbole to drive home his point) and more zealous in obedience to all the laws than anyone else. Indeed, Peter and James, the leaders of the congregation in Jerusalem, wanted to restrict membership in their group to Jews. Any non-Jew or Gentile who wished to join first had to be converted to Judaism, and could later apply for membership in the Church.

58

Inevitably an ever-widening gulf grew between the two religions. Within a matter of decades in the Common Era, if not sooner, the two groups parted company, although the Christians continued to recognize their rich Jewish heritage and maintained a relatively close connection with many of the instructions of the Old Testament, altering them when necessary to fit into their own ethos, doctrine, and dogma.

There may have been another reason why an intentional choice was made for a different day of worship. Ever since the Romans had conquered Israel in the century before Christ, an attempt had been made to regain independence. At least two of Jesus' own disciples, Simon the Zealous and Judas Iscariot (Judas the Sicarii—a member of an underground terrorist group that assassinated Romans and their Jewish collaborators), were among those who sought freedom. Indeed, according to some traditions outside the Gospels, one of the more serious charges against Jesus was that he was an insurrectionist who had encouraged others to rebel against both Rome and the Jewish law. Yet, when war came in AD 66, at the outbreak of the First Jewish Revolt, many Christians were quick to proclaim that this was not their war and that they had nothing to do with the Jews. From Luke's Gospel, written about that time, it is clear that blame for Jesus' death had been shifted from the Romans to the Jews. It is possible that the early Christians intentionally emphasized Sunday as their day of worship as another means of distinguishing themselves from the Jews.

Thus, the precedent was established that continues to the present time: Sunday, the Lord's Day, became a time of recreation and re-creation for the individual. It was a time for Christians to gather together for worship, and as we shall see, until the late sixteenth century, the afternoon was often given over to pleasurable activities.

We see this more playful or recreational use of the Christian holy day in England after the arrival of William the Conqueror in 1066. The new Norman king believed it was his sacred duty to protect the Church. After all, had it not been for the express permission and encouragement of the Pope and the Church, he never would have been able to initiate his invasion of Saxon England. At the same time, he believed the Church should serve as the arsenal of defense for the nation. Establishing a new precedent, he ordered all monastic houses and convents to maintain and support knights and their retainers and infantrymen. All parish churches were required to plant and cultivate yew trees— the raw materials of which were made into the famous long bows and arrows necessary to wage war or defend the nation from invaders. On summer Sunday afternoons (during the long season of Whitsuntide—now called Pentecost or Trinity in many Anglican and Episcopal churches), all able-bodied men of the parish were expected to report for drill duty, archery practice, and later, musket practice. Then, once their commanders were satisfied with the day's drill, all adjourned to the nearest public house (pub) for one or more pints of Whitsuntide ale. No doubt many men were far more interested in drinking and talking than in studying the manual of arms and practicing target shooting.

G. Corwin Stoppel

Sunday afternoons in England were also the time when Morris dancers enjoyed their hobby and children danced around a Maypole, carrying on traditions dating back to pagan times. On major feast days, a feast would be held in the churchyard or elsewhere in the village or community, a precursor of our own potluck dinners. In some of the larger cities, there were morality plays, jugglers, dancers, and other forms of public recreation. In short, Sunday mornings were devoted to worship, afternoons to fun and relaxation.

But one Sunday afternoon, pleasure came to an abrupt halt during the English Reformation. The more conservative Protestants, including the separatists (i.e., those who wanted to completely separate Church from state, end the temporal power of the bishops, and have a congregational style of worship and polity), were appalled at what they saw. People were drinking, playing, and worst of all, having fun on the one day religious conservatives believed should be solemnly observed. Often taking their text from the Old Testament, these conservatives were opposed to the use of alcohol, believing that it led to a lowering of inhibitions and to sexual improprieties, swearing, and violence. Dancing, they thought, was little more than a prelude to sexual immorality. They believed that military drill, although necessary to defend and advance the cause of the Church Militant, should not be done on Sundays. Dancing around a Maypole was not just a harmless child's activity, but a re-enactment of pagan worship at the ashrams and other forbidden "high places" of the Old Testament era. Indeed, they believed that all forms of pleasure and recreation on Sunday were wrong, for it should be a day given over to attending church, Bible study, prayer, hymn singing, and devotion to God. All forms of recreation were suspect as nothing other than opportunities for Satan to capture the unwary soul. And recreation, especially on Sunday, violated the spirit, if not the letter, of this commandment. They demanded an immediate return to the precepts of the Old Testament, albeit on Sundays and not on Saturdays.

Their ultimate goal was to create a Christian, Old Testament–style theocracy. When the Puritans moved to

Massachusetts in the 1620s, and when their counterparts took control of England in the 1640s and 1650s, they began imposing their theology and ethos on the people. In both England and New England, there was strict enforcement of the Sunday laws. Church attendance at morning and afternoon worship services was mandatory, and anyone who missed the worship without good cause could be severely fined or punished. Anyone caught lighting a fire, cooking, or enjoying themselves in any way was in violation of those laws.

Their rationale was as simple as their opponents thought it was misguided: Life was real, life was earnest, hell was an ever-present threat, and it was the responsibility of all humanity to honor and serve God at all times and in all places and things. Any form of frivolity, even too much smiling or laughter—especially when done on the Lord's Day—was deemed offensive to God, an opportunity for the devil to make inroads, and must therefore be suppressed. Those rules and regulations were drawn together in what became known as the Blue Laws.

In a theocracy, a near-theocracy, or a very homogenous culture, it is sometimes possible for sacred and secular leaders to impose this type of regulation on people because the majority, or at least a very powerful minority, gives their consent. Although there might be some grumbling and complaining about the restrictions, on the whole everyone is more or less obedient, willing to forgo some of their rights and freedoms for what they believe to be the higher good of their society and the worship of God. However, few individuals or groups are able to maintain a high level of religious fervor for more than a few years, and such a theocracy rarely lasts for more than a generation. Despite stern warnings from the "true believers" and the more conservative and zealous members, other factors and interests intervene and passion diminishes. In New England the Puritan theocracy lasted for less than two decades. By then immigrants, many of whom did not subscribe to the Puritans' beliefs and mores, moved into the region and eventually became the majority.

G. Corwin Stoppel

However, neither the formal separation of Church and state, nor a constitutional amendment forbidding the government from establishing a church or even endorsing and supporting a particular religion prevented a deeply influential relationship between the secular and the sacred. Government and secular law, to a certain extent, regulate what churches can and cannot do; likewise, religious communities have a great impact on laws and public policies. Often the two clusters of institutions work well together; at other times sharp disagreements can only be resolved by the courts.

A community's Sunday closing laws make this disagreement particularly apparent. For years many communities forbade any nonessential business from being open on Sunday, while others controlled what goods or services could be provided. A hardware store might not be allowed to be open on Sunday, but gasoline stations, restaurants, and small convenience stores could be. Some communities have passed ordinances that forbid the sale of alcohol, tobacco, and other nonessential products, while allowing the sale of milk and other food. In some small communities, local customs frown on those who mow their lawns, work in their gardens, play outside, or make too much noise on Sunday.

62

Gradually, as new people move into those smaller communities, or as organized religion begins to loosen its grip, residents re-examine the old Sunday closing laws. Voters ponder why they cannot buy alcohol in their community, but can drive a few miles to another town to make their purchases. Business owners seek to have the local ordinances changed so they will not lose customers. Even those businesses that once welcomed Sunday as a day off from work find it increasingly necessary to open their doors to satisfy their customers.

Compounding the challenge is our increasingly multicultural society in which Christians and non-Christians live and work side by side. Sometimes non-Christians or members of other religions who do not recognize Sunday as a day of worship and rest raise legal objections to the Sunday closing laws. That has led some of the more conservative Christians to lament that we are now living in a post-Christian era, or that the United States is no longer a "Christian" nation, as they imagined it to have been in the past. We are challenged to understand how we can accommodate Muslims who want Friday as their day of worship, Jews and some Christian groups who want Saturday, and Christians who claim Sunday. Should the majority prevail in a neighborhood or community? Or, should the minority be allowed to dictate to the majority? Should Christians in a predominantly Islamic neighborhood or community be forced to observe Muslim holy days and holidays?

We do not have simple solutions to those questions. So I suggest we return to the story of Jesus pointing out that the Sabbath was made for humans, not humans for the Sabbath. We can interpret this commandment as God's gift to us. How we balance our lives, how we make room for both work and recreation, how we fulfill our responsibilities to ourselves, our families, our church, our community, and God are, I believe, far more important than the day on which we take our rest and worship God. To spend the day working at our job or furthering our career is perhaps not the most appropriate way of keeping the Sabbath—nor is wasting it in meaningless activities or abject sloth. If we spend the day in bed, watching television nonstop, or investing our time and energy in something that does not bring us true, lasting joy, then of what real benefit is this gift? We have abused it. Conversely, if we come to the end of the day and find true joy and satisfaction in our hearts, the knowledge that we have lived each moment to the fullest and can honestly stand before God in gratitude for the day of rest, we have made wise choices.

63

It is for this reason that many Christians make the intentional choice to be at worship on Sundays. By choosing to set aside their work and other activities for a short time, they find themselves renewed and inspired to tackle the challenges they face during the rest of the week. In part, it is fulfilling our need to worship God; in part, it is hearing and responding to Jesus' invitation to put his precepts into practice. For many Christians, communal worship is

G. Corwin Stoppel

also a reminder that we cannot compartmentalize our life between the secular and the sacred; all our life is of a piece and can be an offering to God.

Yet, to compel or to be compelled to attend a worship service accomplishes nothing either, because the individual is either focusing attention on something else or is angry that he or she must be present. So we revel in our liberty to attend worship because we truly want to be there.

This commandment gives us latitude in discerning and putting into practice the means by which we will honor and worship God and at the same time refresh our hearts, bodies, and minds. The important thing is that we opt to do it.

◆

64

✦

Beyond Flowers and Power Tools

THE FIFTH COMMANDMENT

Honor thy father and thy mother.

W HEN ASKED WHICH COMMANDMENT was the most important, Jesus said, "'You shall love the Lord your God with all your heart, and with all your soul, and with all your mind.' This is the greatest and first commandment. And a second is like it: 'You shall love your neighbor as yourself.' On these two commandments hang all the law and the prophets" (Matthew 22:37–40). His response corresponds to the division of the Ten Commandments: The first four spell out our relationship with God and our responsibility to God; the rest describe how we are to relate to other people and things.

I find this commandment to be the most optimistic, positive, inspiring, and idealistic. It presupposes a good reason for us to honor our parents, that they are honorable people to begin with, and that they are therefore worthy of our devotion. It implies something inherently good about our mothers and fathers, encouraging us to search out those attributes worthy of honor or remembrance—even if it takes considerable searching! This commandment also invokes the highest ideals of love and respect in a parent-child relationship. It calls for much more than a nod of gratitude on Mother's or Father's Day.

In the ancient world, a father typically had absolute power over his children. In many cultures throughout the Mediterranean basin and the Middle East, his rights were considered to be divinely ordained. From the moment of birth, a father had absolute power of life and death over his sons and daughters. If, for example, the child was born with deformities, if there were already too many children in the household, if the baby was a girl instead of the much more prized son, for whatever reason or for no reason at all, the father could kill the child or have it killed, often by abandoning the child to wild animals or the gods, as happened famously to Oedipus and to Romulus and Remus.

In the lengthy Old Testament saga of Abraham and Sarah, we see that it was Sarah who attempted to do away with her stepson, Ishmael. Because Sarah had not been able to conceive a child (again, preferably a son), she had followed the ancient practice of giving her slave girl, Hagar, to her husband to father a child who could then carry on the family name and inherit his estate. Later, when Sarah bore Isaac, Hagar and Ishmael were not only expendable but a liability. Ishmael was a constant reminder of her husband's relationship with Hagar, and there was always the possibility that he, rather than her own son, Isaac, could inherit all that Abraham possessed. Ultimately Sarah could have been dispossessed and even abandoned by her stepson. Had Abraham not rescued Hagar and Ishmael, they would have perished in the wilderness.

Sometime later it is Abraham who is fully prepared to make a human sacrifice of his son, Isaac. According to the Book of Genesis, Abraham and Isaac, and several men in Abraham's employ, traveled from their camp to the end of the Kidron Valley, now directly beneath the Old City of Jerusalem. The people of the region had been performing human sacrifices for many generations at Gehenna—a name that means "the gateway to hell." Abraham built an altar, laid wood on it, and was ready to kill his child with his knife when an angel commanded him to stop. Though both of these stories are open to multiple interpretations, they clearly remind us that parents had the power of life and death over their children.

The father continued to wield tremendous power over his children even as they grew older. A child could be sold into slavery, executed, given away to another to pay off all or part of a debt, consigned to a pagan temple where he or she might be trained to become a priest or a priestess or made into a cult prostitute, or given in marriage to cement an alliance between two families or to reduce the burden on the family to provide for her. As long as the father was alive, his will prevailed.

Instructions in the Torah say that a parent has the right, if not the responsibility, to execute a child who is willfully disobedient or "talks back" to her or his parents. It is unclear whether that law was ever employed, but its very existence re-emphasizes the extent of parental rights. In the Wisdom literature (including Proverbs, Ecclesiastes, and some of the Psalms) and in the Apocrypha, we find additional instructions for parent-child relationships. Just as children have the solemn responsibility to honor, obey, and respect their parents, parents are to teach their children right from wrong, and, if necessary, punish them physically or await the consequences. The proverb "Spare the rod and spoil the child" is perhaps best known among those short teachings, and the rape of Tamar is particularly remembered among the longer Old Testament sagas.

The tragedy begins in King David's palace when one of his sons rapes his half-sister, Tamar. Tamar's brother, Absalom, learns of Amnon's offense and spends the next several years nursing his anger and hatred and plotting his revenge. Throughout those long years, Tamar is further victimized by being told by her family to keep quiet about the sexual assault. Absalom finally murders his half-brother, then flees into exile for several years before finally being allowed to return home to Jerusalem. However, David is still so angry that Absalom committed murder and made public their family's disgrace that he refuses to speak to him or allow him into his presence. The rift between father and son continues to grow until it erupts into a full-fledged rebellion that sends David and his courtiers fleeing the capital for their lives.

The rebellion was short-lived; in a single battle, Absalom's army was defeated. Absalom fled for his life, but his long hair became ensnared in a tree branch. While hanging from the branch, David's general, Joab, and a small band of soldiers killed Absalom—despite the instructions from the king that no harm should come to his son.

Although relieved to retain his throne, David mourned the loss of his son and commissioned a tomb to be built in his memory. Absalom's tomb can still be seen in the Kidron Valley (not far from Gehenna, where Abraham was prepared to sacrifice his son Isaac). For centuries fathers have taken their sons to this site, encouraged them to throw a small stone at the tomb, and used it as an object lesson about the dangers of rebelling against one's father and leading a wicked life.

As children grew older, their fathers still made all decisions for them and held dominion over them, though for the most part, daughters fared far worse than sons. When a daughter reached maturity, a father let the community know he was accepting offers from parents who had sons of marriageable age. That tradition continues even today among the Bedouin people living in Israel and elsewhere in the Middle East. The parents place a white flag over their tent to inform the community they are willing to negotiate an arranged marriage for their daughter. It remains the father's prerogative to decide who his daughter will marry and when; her wishes are of little importance. Nor, for that matter, were the wishes of the son always taken into consideration in arranged marriages.

Even after a son or daughter married, they were never able to completely escape parental authority. Unless the son moved to another location, when he married he was expected to bring his wife to his father's house, tent, or village, and continue to work in his father's fields, tend his flocks, or work in the family business. The son's emancipation came only if he moved away or at his father's death. Only then did he become a man in his own right.

A daughter, for her part, was taken in hand by her mother-in-law after marrying. Under her guidance and sometimes domination, the young wife continued to learn how to cook, clean, and sew, and was expected to produce a steady stream of babies. The wife who could not bear children or did not produce sons was held in the lowest esteem by her husband and his family, and might possibly suffer death at their hands. Only when her mother-in-law died did the daughter become the family's matriarch and gain any true sense of freedom.

For most of us in the West, this seems like a dreadful way to live. We prefer to marry for love rather than a "bride price," and we tend to prize our personal happiness above all else. Even when an individual marries in hope of financial benefit or elevated social status, or to escape loneliness or abuse, the expectation is that the union will improve our happiness. However, marriage as being about the pursuit of love and happiness was something almost unknown and even unimaginable in a culture where mere survival—including through producing many children—was of paramount importance.

That type of highly structured family system, where nearly all power was vested in the hands of a father, was always ripe for abuse. Though we can assume that most parents were loving, without laws nothing could stop a sadistic, wicked, or violent father from doing whatever he wished.
69

The ancient Jews were not the only ones whose culture so highly valued respect and honor toward parents. Socrates and Plato, ancient Greece's finest philosophical minds, were firmly committed to the high idealism of honoring one's parents. In addition to treating parents with the same respect accorded to a member of the nobility, a priest, or a teacher-philosopher, they saw an implied duty: Children's honor and respect of their parents was the principle way of thanking parents for their care during the children's formative years, and that respect included caring for one's parents in their old age. Reverential children saw to it that their parents lacked for nothing that was in their means to provide, which included not only the basic necessities of life but also time and attention.

For the Greeks the idealistic relationship between parents and children was an extension of their quest for the

G. Corwin Stoppel

balanced, good, and happy life. Indeed, the Greeks sought the highest standards in all things, whether it was the performing and visual arts or the Olympic Games. Their standards of behavior were based not on a strict legal code but on a sense of duty, obligation, and mutual responsibility, which a good person was expected to embrace for its own sake.

The Romans, who eventually conquered the Greeks and borrowed heavily from their culture, took things one step further. Gravitas, or seriousness, was the underlying foundation of all Roman philosophy, whether in politics or the family. To be certain that every child conformed to the high idealism of respect and honor for one's parents, laws mandated obedience. Any son, regardless of his wealth or power, was subject to his father's decisions, and no law would provide for a son's appeal to a higher authority. If the lowest, most wicked peasant anywhere in the empire ordered his son put to death for whatever reason, not even the emperor could intervene.

◆

70

Jesus grew up in a culture that was highly influenced by these three important sources: the teachings of the rabbis and Judaism, Greek philosophy and idealism, and strict Roman law. We see those sources influencing how Jesus grew up and related to his parents, most notably in the story of his presentation in the Temple. Here he seems less than obedient and respectful to his parents. Walking home with others after Jesus' presentation, Mary and Joseph discover to their horror that Jesus is not with the group. After several days of what must have been a frenzied, frightful, and frantic search in Jerusalem, they find Jesus in the Temple talking with the most learned men of his day—the elders. When his parents question why he did not stay with the party, Jesus' response is less than respectful, "Did you not know you would find me in my Father's house?"

We are left to speculate on Jesus' formative years, for the Bible tells us nothing of the time between the presentation and Jesus' baptism in the Jordan River by his distant cousin John. Several scholars have suggested that he spent his time working in the carpenter's shop, providing for his family after the death of Joseph, but that is pure speculation and perhaps wishful thinking on our part. We only pick up his story two decades later at the wedding feast in Cana, where we find Jesus answering his mother sharply when she points out that the host has run out of wine. When she intimates that he should do something, he tells her that it is none of his concern—yet immediately he turns the water into good wine.

Sometime later, when told that his mother, brothers, and sisters are asking for him, Jesus makes a comment that seemingly disowns them—"Who is my mother or my brothers or my sisters?"—and then explains that his family are those who do the will of the Father. And yet, at the very end of his life as he is dying on the cross, he shows great compassion for his mother by entrusting her well-being to one of the disciples: "Woman, behold your son," he says to his mother, and to the disciple, "Behold your mother."

As we search for biblical models to live out this commandment, I suggest we look beyond specific laws and their attendant punishments and retributions to our freedom in Christ, our freedom—rather than our duty—to love, and the grace for living that comes through Christ. Then instead of a strict obedience to laws, instead of trying to live up to the almost impossibly high idealism of the Greek culture, Christians fulfill this commandment because they want to do so. As part of their response to God's grace, obedience to, honor for, and respect of parents become a joyful privilege. Instead of a dire fear of punishment for less than perfection, we have a passionate desire to honor God by keeping this commandment. It is a complete reversal of the old status quo.

In Christ there is a radical shift in the relationship between parent and child. Now there is mutual obligation and responsibility. To be certain, children still have the duty of honoring and respecting their parents, but at the same time, the parents' responsibility toward their children is primarily of giving love. Simply giving birth to a child, providing for his or her basic material needs, and allowing the child to grow up into an adult are no longer sufficient.

◆
71

G. Corwin Stoppel

We find ourselves caught between the idealistic state of perfection and reality. Our goal has always been to create and support loving families where care and mutual respect are found between parents and their children. In the back of our minds, we would like all families to appear as if they stepped out of a Norman Rockwell painting. The whole family troops off together to church, enjoys an intergenerational meal together, plays fairly, and takes delight in simple pleasures. To that ideal we have added images from popular 1950s and 1960s television programs such as *Father Knows Best* and *Leave It to Beaver.* Yet, we find those romanticized ideals light years from reality. The daily dose of tragic news deflates us as we learn about broken families, abandoned children, and child and elder abuse. Such news beaks our hearts, even though there is nothing new about it. Perhaps the greatest difference is that we more openly discuss those problems today than in the past.

Our contemporary society recognizes those problems and searches for solutions. Over the past century, government involvement has increased in the protection and care of children and in support for families of all types. In the past, schools saw their exclusive function to be to provide education; today greater emphasis is placed on holistic care of children and parents. In the past if parents abused their children, it was often considered a private matter or a neighborhood scandal. In some cases the men of the community might "re-educate" the abusers with their fists; today suspected child or elder abuse is a matter for the authorities. We have also become increasingly wary of others—not just the stranger offering a ride or candy to children, but even members of our own family, community, and church.

For all this preventive community action, much of the harm done to children still occurs in their own homes, at the hands of their parents. So the question remains: How can we honor and respect an absent, violent, abusive, or just plain bad mother or father? How can we honor them if they have proven themselves unworthy of that honor and devotion? Indeed, should we? Under the Old Testament laws, as well as in Rome and Greece, the behavior of the parent was immaterial. The law was clear: A child must give honor and respect to her or his parents no matter how unworthy they might be. In the new covenant in Christ is a clear sense of mutual responsibility. A parent wishing to be honored and respected by her or his children must be a person of honor and worthy of respect. Perhaps, then, the best we can hope for in these unpleasant or less than perfect situations is to keep focused on the ideal of a good parent and the attributes to which such a mother or father would aspire.

We also find ourselves blessed by those individuals who, because they are sensitive to the challenges of contemporary society or because they have been harmed in the past, intentionally choose to take positive action. They volunteer their time as mentors or counselors or working with youth groups or the elderly. Realizing that they cannot solve all the problems of the world or even all the problems of their own community, they do what they can where they are. For them, living out this commandment is a matter of practical, practicing Christianity.

◆

73

Over two centuries ago, John Wesley noted that Christianity knows nothing of solitary religion. So what can we do, as a Church, to live out this commandment together? Our work begins by making certain our parishes are family friendly and supportive. Here at All Saints' in Saugatuck, Michigan, our children periodically take an active role in worship, such as by reading the lessons or leading the Prayers of the People. We encourage all adults, not just parents, to visit the Sunday school rooms during the coffee hour and let the children show and tell what they have been doing. When parents and others clearly see that the entire parish family is concerned about a child's formation in its widest possible scope, parents quickly follow its lead.

It begins with such simple things as being tolerant of children who may make a bit of noise or movement during a worship service, instead of sending hostile glares or critical comments, or shushing them. More than once, when some children were making a bit of noise during the sermon, I have stopped and deliberately, publicly reassured an

G. Corwin Stoppel

anxious or embarrassed parent by saying, "It's wonderful hearing the sound of a child in church." I believe that type of leadership is essential in building up the whole body of Christ, not just the adult body. The concern for children continues with inviting young children to help serve as greeters, thereby being able to take visiting children and their parents back to the Sunday school. It continues with encouraging children to serve as acolytes, and not criticizing them for mistakes they may make while performing their duties. It means spending time with parents and sponsors (godparents, as they are still called in some parishes) prior to Holy Baptism so that they understand the significance and seriousness of the vows they are making.

Just as important, it means spending time with the entire congregation so they understand their vows of support and assistance to parents in bringing up their children in a Christian environment. For example, this winter our deacon met several times during the Sunday school hour with eight young children, preparing them for taking their First Communion. On the fourth Sunday of Lent, also known as Mothering Sunday, the young members took Communion for the first time, received certificates from the church, and were feted at a coffee hour. Likewise, an entire congregation can imaginatively embrace and support the Christian education program by helping teachers and parents, expressing appreciation for all that they do, spending time with the children in their Sunday school classroom and throughout the church, and finding tangible means of letting them know how important they are in the parish family. And, when necessary, gently correcting them so that they learn to do the right things.

For a parish to take this commandment seriously means creating and maintaining an active program for teenagers and young adults, offering classes and workshops for new parents, providing counseling and referrals when necessary, and, when it is appropriate, offering support and reassurance to parents whose children have chosen to take what seems to be a destructive and self-destructive course.

At the same time, a parish has the responsibility of creating and maintaining a way to support adult children so that they can fulfill their responsibilities to their parents inherent in this commandment. That can be a challenging issue for many young and middle-aged adults as their parents grow older. Trying to balance the responsibilities of their own families and working lives and the desire to care for parents with ever-increasing medical and sometimes financial needs can be highly stressful. Overwhelmed, some adult children abdicate their responsibilities; others attempt to do too much—to the detriment of their own families, health, jobs, and finances. Most are burdened with a sense of guilt, in particular if they are arranging to relocate a mother or a father from their home to a nursing-care facility or agreeing on end-of-life decisions. Here, the church has an opportunity to offer guidance, support, and empathy to those adults who are doing their best to make the right decisions.

We also believe that this work must be done outside the church. Several years ago, when the local Congregational Church began an after-school project to reach out to children who didn't play sports, we volunteered our financial support. Before long some of our members were actively participating in the project. And this year our chapter of the Brotherhood of St. Andrew designated the proceeds from our Shrove Tuesday pancake dinner and the Lenten love offering boxes to this work.

Finally, there is the challenge of obeying this commandment after one's parents have died. In the ideal situation, children are left with a rich legacy of happy memories; high idealism of service to God, family, and community; and a clear sense of moral direction. Theodore Roosevelt, for example, when faced with difficult decisions, often wondered what his father would do, pondered on that question, and then took what he believed to be the right course of action. He claimed that when he followed that method, he was rarely wrong.

Many years ago George Gibbs, my sixth-grade Sunday school teacher, somehow managed to collect a picture of each child's parents and put it in an envelope for each of us, along with a one- and a five-dollar bill. When he gave us our envelopes, he said that we were not to spend the money. Rather, anytime we had a tough decision to make, we were to take out the envelope and look at the contents, then ask ourselves if it was something of which "Honest Abe," President Washington, and our parents would approve. If it was, then it was the right thing to do; if we had any doubts, we needed to reconsider our decision. Some four decades later, that guidance stays with me.

After my father died, Mother cleaned out his billfold and found two one-hundred-dollar bills. She gave one to my sister and one to me. Accompanying the bill was a brief note explaining that Dad always kept those bills in reserve, just in case of an emergency or if he could do something extraordinary for his family. I framed my bill and the note, not as an icon from my late father but as a reminder to carry on the tradition.

Other children, unfortunately, are not blessed with such good memories of their parents. One woman told me that she could never say the Lord's Prayer or anything in reference to God the Father because of the brutal treatment she had received from her father. A male image of God was anathema to her. Many have been able to find release from the past through prayer, counseling, and in some instances, long-term therapy. Mercifully, some have been able to internalize that not all parents are hurtful and wicked, and can use those conclusions to establish the pattern for their own life, as well as to clearly understand what they do not want to do to their own children. By God's grace they have been able to break the pattern of abuse and become parents worthy of their children's honor and respect.

Today many families face the additional challenge of maintaining a long-distance relationship. Whereas in the past, one generation lived close to the next, sometimes even sharing the same house or farm, today it is far more common for children to move hundreds, even thousands, of miles from home. At the same time, it is not unusual for parents to retire in some of the warmer regions of the country, leaving their children and grandchildren behind. How do we honor parents in circumstances such as those?

One way is through making a concerted effort to maintain the lines of communication. Whether it is through e-mail, snail mail, or the telephone; through periodic visits; or by keeping alive family traditions, adult children find the means to stay in contact with their parents and give them the reassurance of their love and devotion. So we find ways, through our changing lives and situations, to creatively honor our parents, and in so doing, provide an example for the children in our care to do the same.

✦

G. Corwin Stoppel

CHAPTER SIX

✦

Taking Stock of Taking Life

THE SIXTH COMMANDMENT

Thou shall commit no murder.

ALMOST DAILY THE NEWS brings us stories of killings in various parts of the Middle East and elsewhere in the world—even in seemingly safe and placid Sweden, where the foreign minister was assassinated—including the ongoing wars in Iraq and Afghanistan and the suicide bombers in Israel. Men and women in uniform in those combat zones come from each of our communities, and we are anxious for their safety. As I write this, recent weeks have brought constant reports about the terrorist train attack in Madrid; today we hear dire warnings from the government about possible deadly terrorist attacks before the November elections in this country. Before that it was the highway sniper in Ohio, the D.C. shooters, and the shooting spree at the Columbine, Colorado, high school, and on and on. . . . We are relieved to have survived another day, and yet also complacent: With acts of violence and homicides so numerous, we know what Stalin meant when he said that a million deaths is a statistic, but one death is a tragedy.

The root causes of murder and mass homicide have sickening similarities: fear, jealousy, anger, greed, revenge, lust, and unbridled rage. Whether it is two nations fighting over natural resources or the acquisition of land, or two neighbors arguing over some alleged slight, too often violent death is the result. In turn we become increasingly wary of strangers and people who are different from ourselves or whose race or ethnic background makes us anxious. We build gated communities to keep strangers at a distance, and we stand in long lines to go through metal detectors at airports, sporting events, and schools. We surrender many of our civil rights in the hope of greater personal and national security. We worry about friends and family members when they leave for work in the morning, anxious for their safe return.

This is no way to live, and we know it. This is not what God wants for us. This is not the abundant life for which Jesus came among us. We yearn for a safer, kinder, gentler era when people did not constantly fear for their safety. Yet, such a time never existed.

The simple existence of ancient legal codes shows that murder existed from well before the historic era. All of them forbade the wanton taking of life; all of them prescribed the harshest penalties for committing murder.

As interesting as it might be to survey the ancient laws of different cultures, here we want to focus only on Judaism. When we read the legal code found in the Torah, we find a number of laws prohibiting the taking of human life, as well as the punishment for that offense—execution. The reason for the laws was simple. Men and women are created in the image of God; human life, therefore, is considered so precious that the punishment for wantonly and intentionally taking the life of another person must be harsh. However, as we know from the news, it is not always clear whether a death was intentional, accidental, or done in a moment of anger. For example, several years ago we heard the tragic story of a woman in the Chicago suburbs with a long history of clinical depression, a woman in the process of an acrimonious divorce, who suffered a mental breakdown and poisoned and suffocated her children. It came on the heels of a story a year earlier of a woman from Texas who broke under the strains of an abusive husband, postpartum depression, trying to homeschool five young children, and trying to maintain the pretense of having a

◆
80

"perfect" life. Many others are living such lives of quiet desperation, perhaps one crisis away from snapping.

Precisely because life is so precious and because the punishment is so harsh and permanent, there had to be strict rules about when the death penalty was to be applied. When the Israelites reclaimed the Holy Land following the Exodus, six cities were designated as places of refuge or sanctuary. When we look at the place names and locations, we see that they were carefully spread across the country so that no one was more than a day's journey away from one of them. If someone took another's life, they had the right to flee to one of the cities of refuge. Once there, and having reported to the local officials to claim sanctuary, no one could apprehend them and take them away for summary execution or punishment. Indeed, it was the responsibility of the officials to protect them from harm. However, these were not cities filled with murderers and other criminals living together in community. Rather, before the accused could be taken away, the city officials held a hearing to determine whether the death with accidental, intentional, premeditated, or committed in a moment of passion. If the death had been intentional or premeditated, the offender could be taken out of the city for punishment or execution. If the death was accidental, or even if it was committed in the heat of the moment, the accused could not be forced to leave the city with the accusers for what would most certainly be her or his execution.

81

The laws regulating the hearing were also strict and demanded the evidence of two credible eyewitnesses. The ancient Israelites did not believe in circumstantial evidence or mere hearsay, much less speculation. The eyewitnesses were individually questioned, and if their stories matched, the judges had the evidence they needed to convict and sentence the offender. If the stories did not match, the accused could not be executed.

Furthermore, because life was deemed so precious, even the method of execution was prescribed by law so that it would be as quick and humane as possible. Whereas other cultures sought to torture and prolong the agony of death, the Israelites retained respect even for the condemned

G. Corwin Stoppel

felon. The person to be executed could be stoned, burned, strangled, or beheaded. That may sound barbaric to us, but when compared to other forms of execution, such as drawing and quartering, crucifixion, or slowly torturing the person to death, those were considered to be humane forms of execution. Originally, stoning was done by taking the individual to a cliff and tossing him onto the rocks below. If the fall did not kill him, those present threw rocks on top of him until he was dead. Later the Jews adopted the foreign practice of taking the individual to the walls outside their city and throwing stones at the person until he was knocked unconscious and then killed. Burning was carried out by burying the condemned man in dried animal waste, using a cloth to hold open his mouth, and then pouring molten metal down his throat. Those who were to be strangled to death or beheaded were tied to a post so that when they died, their bodies did not fall on the ground—something believed to be offensive to both God and their fellow citizens. After the convicted criminal was dead, the body was buried rather than left on display, as was the tradition in other cultures.

◆

As gruesome as those forms of execution may sound to us, compared to the methods used in other countries (particularly by the Romans, who employed crucifixion; or the Greeks, who used slow-acting poison; or other nations that found barbarous ways of executing their condemned), Jewish executions were remarkably humane. However, those laws were the ideal, and as we repeatedly read throughout the Old Testament, many times the people fell far short of what was expected of them.

In addition, execution was permitted only when the murder had been premeditated or intentional. If it was an accidental death, unintentional homicide, or even the result of an act of passion, the individual was not necessarily executed. Nor were the survivors allowed to extract revenge by murdering the person, and/or his family, that they deemed responsible for the loss of life. Rather, they were expected to negotiate a price to settle the family's loss.

As we will note later, death was sometimes the punishment for offenses other than murder.

In the New Testament, we find a radical shift in theology because Jesus has given us a new interpretation of this commandment. When someone asked him about taking the life of another person, Jesus replied that if we so much as hate another man or woman to the extent that we wish they were dead, then we are already as guilty of committing murder as if we had actually done the deed. His response not only intensifies and greatly magnifies the seriousness of the sixth commandment, but also re-emphasizes the sacredness of all human life as a gift from God. By studying the Lord's interpretation of this commandment, we gain far greater insight into many of the problems of our society.

In the Old Testament, the Jews were bound together by their goal of adhering to the Ten Commandments and the other laws found in the Torah. In the case of this commandment, the law was very specific, but detached. Effectively it said: "If you intentionally commit murder and are apprehended and convicted, you will be put to death. If you commit accidental homicide, here are the things you must do to satisfy the victim's family for their loss and make atonement with God." It was a very simple legal code. In the New Covenant with Jesus, the law is maintained, but added to it are the human and relationship elements. We move from treating people as objects to understanding people as creatures born and loved by God.

Only a sociopath or psychopath can intentionally take the life of another person without feeling any remorse for, or connection with, the victim. In literature one of the finest examples of an individual attempting to live with having committed homicide is found in Dostoevsky's *Crime and Punishment*. But even in this story, the young man who fantasizes about being a superman beyond the confines and authority of the law begins to discover that he cannot live without a conscience. Fortunately, such individuals are rare. Most homicides are committed by those who know or are intimately connected with the victim, and often it is a crime of passion. Therefore, in Jesus' interpretation of the commandment, to allow a relationship to deteriorate to the point where friendship or love becomes brutal anger and hatred is the true root of the problem. For that reason Jesus said that if we hate another person to the point that we wish he or she were dead, we have already convicted ourselves of committing murder. The relationship and intent, rather than the mechanics of the law, are key to the Christian life. We are to constantly and consistently work on our relationships with other people so that we never allow them to deteriorate to the point of hatred, much less murder.

For more specific ideas on how to accomplish that task, we turn to the instructions in the latter portion of nearly all Paul's epistles, as well as the entire Epistle of James. We are commanded to find the tangible means of demonstrating unselfish love. The hungry need to be fed, the naked clothed, the thirsty given something to drink, the destitute supported, and the lonely and hurting comforted through our concern for them. Our task is always to work toward community building and reaching out to others, in part as the means of preventing crimes of passion and murder. Love in action is the finest means of obeying this commandment.

Where relationships have already deteriorated, we once again find our example in the life and teachings of Jesus Christ—in reconciliation. Just as Jesus worked to reconcile the world to God, each of us works on reconciliation with those to whom we are estranged. Despite our best efforts and hardest work, we know that differences do arise between family members and the closest of friends. Sometimes it is because of a misunderstanding, sometimes because outside forces have intervened or interfered, and sometimes because one individual does something that is abhorrent to the other. Whatever the reason may be, the result is a rift. Left unattended, it becomes worse and worse. Gradually the estrangement leads to anger, and anger to hatred and sin. So we work for reconciliation, between individuals, within churches or between denominations, and between nations and races. Here at All Saints' we have one member who is an active participant in a diocesan training program on racism in the Church, our deacon is working on judicial reform and juvenile justice, and we have a number of others who volunteer their time and energy on local committees and organizations that work for reconciliation between people. We invite retired foreign-service officers to give public lectures on the current situation in the Middle East. We commit 4 percent of our revenues to mission outreach work, to help support various agencies that work with the less fortunate, with victims of crime, and with those who experience no end of racial, gender, and ethnic inequalities. That is the work of the Church and its members.

In 1906 President Theodore Roosevelt, from a more secular stance, explained his views on hatred and reconciliation: "The poorest of all emotions for any American to feel is the emotion of hatred toward his fellows. Let him feel a just and righteous indignation where a just and righteous indignation is called for; let him not hesitate to inflict punishment where punishment is needed in the interest of the public; but let him be aware of mere vengeance; and above all, of inciting the masses of the people to such a demand." On paper or in theory, all this looks like a relatively simple task. Our experience has taught us otherwise. It is hard work, yet it is the work to which we have been called.

One area in which progress still needs to be made toward good relations is in business and industry. Think of multiple homicides in businesses and corporations. It has happened so often in U.S. Post Offices that when someone goes into a violent rage at work, we have come to say that they have "gone postal." Investigations of such events typically discover that the perpetrator is either a disgruntled employee under far too much stress or a former employee who seeks revenge for being fired or laid off. Though many companies hire consultants to do psychological interviews of prospective employees to determine whether or not they are likely to become troublemakers or violent, those companies do little to improve the working conditions that incite individuals to commit such violence. Company policies, in an effort to be fair to all, treat employees as objects or work units rather than as individuals. Businesses that

◆
85

work with their employees to address needs and concerns often discover that they enable their employees to be more productive and happier, to the benefit of both the corporate bottom line and the well-being of the employee and his or her family.

That is but one area in which Christians can find the tangible means of putting this commandment into practice.

As we seek to honor this commandment, we are challenged to explore five kinds of murder or killing that are common today: war, capital punishment, suicide, euthanasia, and abortion. With the exception of suicide and euthanasia, unlike homicide, these forms of taking life are corporate rather than individual. A single person cannot decide to go to war. Indeed, even the most despotic tyrant cannot take his or her country to war without at least the tacit consent and aid of the military. Similarly, it is society as a whole that authorizes the execution of convicted criminals. Responsibility is shared in the case of abortion, for although it is a personal decision, it is one that has been sanctioned by society.

86

War. For over seventeen hundred years, Christians have been influenced by Augustine of Hippo's philosophy of a "just war." He considered that all wars could be judged to be either just or unjust. Unjust wars were fought to add more territory to a kingdom, to take the property, resources, or people of another nation for revenge or for other selfish and self-centered motives. Conversely, a just war is waged to right wrongs, to stop a tyrant or an evil leader, or to liberate an enslaved people. In theory Augustine's ideas seem to work quite well. Reality is often quite another matter, for only rarely is a war fought for purely altruistic reasons.

When we look at the wars fought by Americans, we could say that the Revolutionary War was fought to bring liberty to an overtaxed and unrepresented people who were being exploited by the British. The Civil War has long been depicted as the war to emancipate the slaves and preserve the union. Northerners and Southerners alike were willing to take up arms and die for the liberation of human chattel or the right to retain them. For many of the same reasons, the United States entered World War II. In Europe and Asia, totalitarian governments were enslaving conquered peoples and committing genocide. Not responding to their plight—even if Pearl Harbor had not been attacked—would have been immoral. Conversely, we have been guilty of being the aggressor, of waging war usually for the acquisition of additional land, even if the war was justified by other motives. Among those of the nineteenth century were the Mexican-American War, the campaign against the Plains Indians, and the Spanish-American War.

Each war provokes discussion about justification and morality. Among the more controversial American conflicts are the wars in Korea, Vietnam, Panama, and Grenada, and the two Gulf wars. Both supporters and opponents present their views, often polarizing the country. Perhaps the only thing uniting both sides is their keen regret at the loss of life and that politicians and diplomats had not succeeded in preventing them in the first place.

Therein lies the difficulty with St. Augustine's theory on just and unjust war. Reasons and justifications are always murky and confused, come from many different sources, and are seldom crystal clear. It is only after the conflict is over and historians and others are able to look back on the causes of those wars that we can more clearly determine that if there had been negotiations and further attempts at diplomacy, if fear of the unknown had not been a factor, and if vested interests had not intervened, the war could have been avoided. Further, such wars are often the result of domestic politics and the desire to win elections as well as to bolster egos and public perceptions.

Added to that is the frequently heard objection, especially from conservatives in this country, to the United States' involvement with, and sometimes submission to, the United Nations. Even though this organization provides the best and sometimes only means of resolving international disputes, many believe that America's participation in the forum means submitting our interests to foreign powers.

G. Corwin Stoppel

As Christians we find ourselves pulled in several different directions at once. We must first discern whether we believe a war is just or unjust, despite what others attempt to tell us. Many voices are calling to us—it is in the national interest, it is in the interest of preserving the kingdom of Christ, it is for the sake of national security, or it is for some other reason. To complicate matters, the news media have moved from relaying the news to commenting and editorializing, often from the perspective of media owners and in an attempt to raise corporate revenues. That makes it particularly challenging to decide whether the taking of life, even in a supposedly just war, is acceptable.

Fortunately, the American government has traditionally recognized this ambiguity and made allowances for those who are opposed to sanctioned war. Men and women who declare themselves to be conscientious objectors and who can demonstrate that they are making the claim for legitimate reasons, not merely to avoid hardship and danger, have been allowed to participate in alternate forms of service. Some are assigned to civilian jobs; others are conscripted and allowed to serve as noncombatants, often as medics. For some even these alternatives are not acceptable because they believe they would still be supporting the war effort, and these people are left with the choice of either serving time in prison for refusing to obey the law or fleeing the country.

Thus, for many there is no simple solution to the challenge of war in light of this commandment. For others it is a more simple and absolute issue, perhaps best summed up by Stephen Decatur's proclamation, "My country, right or wrong, but my country!" In other words, many believe true patriotism is a matter of obeying the decisions made by the government regardless of one's beliefs or sense of morality. For all it is a matter of discernment, based on their faith and knowledge of God's will for them.

Capital punishment. When we read the ancient law codes from the various civilizations around the world, we soon realize that a number of crimes against either a person or property could be, and often were, punished by execution.

Among them are murder, theft, treason, and rape. The ancient code of Hammurabi listed nearly eighty capital offenses, almost all for crimes against the ruler and the ruling class. The Mosaic laws of ancient Israel also included youthful rebellion against one's parents (even talking back to one's parents!), impersonating or falsely claiming to be a prophet, idolatry, homosexuality, and adultery. In the Dark Ages and the Middle Ages, an era when it was generally accepted that only God could make or depose monarchs (with the consent of the Vicar of Christ, i.e., the Pope), it was a capital offense to even think or dream about the death of the king. Today capital offenses in the United States are most often proposed only as punishment for first-degree murder, and not all states allow the death penalty. In China, however, in addition to murder, rape, and drug dealing, corruption in government or business is also a capital offense.

The purpose of capital punishment has always been to accomplish two goals: to punish the offender and to deter others. Although we do not need to go into detail, until the last century or so, executions were grisly affairs that were intended to be as barbarous and torturous as possible, far more than society's demand of retribution for a serious offense. Those from the upper classes were given the privilege of a swift death. Those from the lower classes or whose crimes were not only an offense against society as a whole but a personal affront to the rulers were made to suffer. Now, with the exception of a few countries in the world, efforts are made to make an execution reasonably humane.

Even so, capital punishment is society's legalization of murder, and that alone is highly offensive to many Christians who believe it is morally wrong. In addition to their opposition to publicly sanctioned murder, many believe that far too many innocent men and women have been put to death in the past or are on death row in penitentiaries today. Further, compelling evidence has shown that the death penalty is more frequently applied to minorities and the poor than to upper- and middle-class whites.

For those who support the death penalty and capital punishment, the question of "why" becomes very important. Some argue that it is in keeping with the laws found in the Old Testament. However, that quickly becomes a weak argument, for few supporters of the death penalty are as scrupulously obedient to other Mosaic laws, such as the prohibitions against eating pork and shellfish or wearing blended-fabric clothing. Nor is it likely that they would wish to see rebellious and disobedient children sent to death row simply for arguing with or talking back to their parents.

Others believe that capital punishment is an appropriate form of revenge. An individual has taken the life of another, therefore that person should be forced to forfeit her or his own life; justice must be served and satisfied. In theory this appears to be a plausible argument, but it is highly questionable whether it works in practice. God warned against seeking revenge, claiming it as his own prerogative. The reason is simple: We are rarely satisfied when we seek revenge. Either we constantly feel the need for extracting even more revenge or we are disappointed that it does not bring us the satisfaction we had anticipated. Not surprisingly, after an execution sympathy often shifts to the condemned person and her or his family.

90

At the same time, some proponents of the death penalty also suggest that life imprisonment with no hope of parole or release is a far greater and less humane punishment than execution. To be certain, our prisons are often crowded and dangerous places, but this argument alone cannot justify capital punishment for those who believe that all life is truly sacred.

Euthanasia. Euthanasia is commonly defined as medically terminating the life of someone who is terminally ill, rather than allowing nature to take its course, which may mean forcing a person to endure what might be great suffering and torment or to linger in what has been called a vegetative state for days, weeks, months, or even years. Euthanasia is usually done under the care of a physician or a practitioner, who administers lethal medications to a dying person. It is radically different from making the decision to turn off the life-support systems that are pumping oxygen into the lungs or making the heart continue to work in a person who is already considered to be brain dead.

The news media keep us keenly aware that over the past two hundred years, medical care has radically advanced and improved. As an example, in the 1820s a strange illness known as Saunder's disease swept through part of Upper Canada (now Ontario). A perfectly health person could be instantly stricken, collapse into a coma, and for all practical purposes, appear to be dead. The problem was that it was difficult to tell if the person had died or was in a coma and would soon recover. However, civil and ecclesiastical law mandated that a person be buried within three days of his or her death. That led to a great fear that a person stricken with Saunder's disease might be buried and then recover while in the grave. To alleviate the fear of burying someone alive—or of being buried alive!—the family cut a hollow reed, inserted it into the coffin lid just above the person's face, and carefully filled in the grave so as not to break or clog the reed. A feather was inserted at the top of the reed, and for the next days and weeks, a family member kept watch to see if the feather had been blown out of the reed. If it had been blown out, the grave was immediately reopened and the person helped out of the coffin. If at the end of the year the feather was still in place, the reed was broken at ground level, a cork was inserted, and a final memorial service was said in an unofficially sanctioned rite known as "corking the reed."

91

Today, thanks to technological advancements, the fear of something like Saunder's disease is a thing of the past, and we no longer have to wonder if a person is in a coma or is actually deceased. Technological progress has made it possible to determine if a person is brain dead; in other words, the brain no longer functions at a sufficient level to give instruction for the heart, lungs, and other vital organs to function, and there is no hope, short of a miracle, that the person will be restored to life. When this has been determined by a physician, and more frequently by a team of physicians, the family is advised to cease heroic efforts and "pull the plug." Breathing tubes and other equipment are removed, and the individual is pronounced dead.

That is radically different from euthanasia, where medications are used to stop the heart and lungs from functioning and bring about death.

Those who advocate euthanasia claim that we treat our pet animals, or any animal in great pain, far more humanely than we treat people. If a dog or cat, no matter how beloved, is suffering from an irreversible illness, a veterinarian often administers an injection of drugs to bring about a quiet, painless, and merciful death. Advocates of human euthanasia believe the same principle should be applied to those who are terminally ill, rather than forcing them to linger and suffer. Family members and friends should be allowed to say their final good-byes and to know that their loved one is no longer in agony.

At the outset this seems to make good sense. However, in light of all that we believe God expects from us in the keeping of this commandment, and what Jesus taught by word and example during his ministry, the legalization of euthanasia raises serious difficulties. We have not addressed the question of who will make the decisions for euthanasia nor the circumstances under which it can be administered.

92

For example, are we willing to "put down" someone who is elderly and suffering from dementia, a severely handicapped child, or someone who has just been diagnosed with a type of cancer for which there is minimal hope of survival? At what point in the course of an illness is the decision made and the procedure carried out? At the diagnosis? Hours before the end? When?

But then we must take it a step further, asking whether there will be societal pressure for an individual to request euthanasia. Will we get to the point of pressuring an individual to request it so that medical expenses can be kept to a minimum? Will we then begin to advocate euthanasia for someone who is not a "productive member of society"? How will we prevent insurance companies from urging terminally ill subscribers to terminate their life? How will we prevent hospital and nursing-home administrators from advocating euthanasia so that space can be made for another patient? Will we begin to insist on euthanasia for those who have no private medical and long-term care insurance so as to lower our taxes that pay for those services?

The heart of the matter is that the legalization of euthanasia, even the widespread acceptance of it, becomes a slippery slope that could readily lead to mandated mercy killing. Once we begin to accept that concept, we have lost our sense of humanity toward those who are older, in pain and suffering, or on the economic fringes of society.

Suicide. Suicide is the ultimate and permanent resolution of a usually temporary problem or challenge. Although in the past and in other cultures, suicide has been a socially acceptable practice for great personal loss, failure, or shame, within Christianity it has always been morally and legally unacceptable. Indeed, early in the history of the Church, when its members were being harshly oppressed by the Romans and others, a number of zealous men and women eagerly sought martyrdom as a means of gaining immediate admission into heaven. They had taken to heart the promises of the glories of heaven, as well as the Platonic and Pauline philosophy of the immaterial and spiritual being of greater value than the material and the physical body, and they were eager to physically die to be promoted to the greater glory. The sooner they could leave earth and their physical bodies, the sooner they could be in the presence of Jesus and enjoy all the benefits of heaven. So many of them were provoking the authorities or even turning themselves in for arrest and execution that the Church Fathers were forced to put an end to the practice by proclaiming that those who did so forfeited their right to eternal life because they had violated this commandment.

The rejection of suicide early in the history of the Church has firmly established the theology that exists today. It is, very simply, unacceptable. There are those who believe it is the one sin for which there can be no forgiveness, because after one has taken his or her own life, it is impossible to plead for mercy and grace. Others, more lenient in their beliefs, still reject the practice as wrong, but believe God will forgive those who commit suicide because they were obviously so mentally or physically ill that they felt they had no other recourse.

The tragic fact is that suicide is the fourth leading cause of death for those in their late teens through the early thirties. Several reasons for committing suicide have been identified: clinical or chemical depression, the use of illegal substances that cause depression, or such self-hatred and personal torment that no other solution to the problem can be seen. Although we must condemn the act of suicide, we must be scrupulously careful to avoid judging or condemning the person who attempts to take or succeeds at taking her or his own life. It is a matter of hating the sin but loving the sinner. Indeed, Christians have the responsibility of helping to bear one another's burdens and doing all within our power to prevent this tragedy from occurring.

To that end physicians and medical researchers have identified chemical imbalances in the body that cause serious depression. For those suffering from it, it is far more than merely feeling a bit "blue" or "down" for a few hours or even a few days. Rather, it is an overwhelming feeling of utter darkness, the weight of the entire world on one's shoulders, an unending sense of gloom with no hope for improvement. Only the person who has personally experienced it can ever know what it is like to live that way, to know the hopelessness and isolation it creates. Fortunately, some medications do help. Unfortunately, antidepressants are not equally effective in all people, and many medications do not become effective until a week or two of doses have accumulated in a person's body. For the person already suffering from depression, that delay and the possibility their medication will not bring relief are debilitating. Even when the medication does work, periodically the dose must be adjusted, and sometimes the medication loses its effectiveness and the whole process must begin anew.

Thus, it becomes our corporate responsibility as Christians to work with those who are suffering from depression, to work for the advancement of medical and

94

psychological care, and to help overcome the stereotype that those suffering from any form of mental illness are to be treated with less dignity and respect than those who have a physical illness.

Some who are suffering depression and considering suicide are attempting to run away from problems or situations that are greatly troubling to them. For young people it might be such things as being bullied at school, questions about their gender identity, problems at home, problems with peer relationships, the inability to live up to the sometimes unreasonable expectations of parents and others whom they admire, a sense of personal failure, or overwhelming shame for something they did or failed to achieve. For all of them, the common thread is that the problems of the moment seemed so great and overwhelming that they saw no other solution but to take their own lives. Others, not willing to commit suicide, might engage in extremely risky or self-destructive behavior so that if they die, it will not appear to others that they have committed suicide and therefore it will not bring shame to their family.

It is here that we are all responsible for offering support to those who are so desperate that they feel nothing is left but to take their own lives.

95

Suicide has a tremendously negative impact on everyone connected to the person who took his or her own life. In my first church, two parishioners committed suicide. One was a middle-aged man who snapped during an extremely long and snowy winter. Every morning and afternoon he had to plow out his half-mile driveway, cutting through drifts that were well over six feet high. One night he apparently decided that it was more than he could take, and he took his life. His family was devastated and hysterical at the news, and then later learned that his suicide voided his insurance policy. Within the year they suffered terrible financial losses. All of us were left wondering what we could or should have done to help him through his emotional agony. The guilt that all the church members, as well as those in the community, felt was overwhelming.

Four years later a high school senior took his life. His family and friends were devastated at their loss, and crushed by their feeling of guilt. They blamed themselves, claiming that they should have been more aware of what was happening in his life, more sensitive to his mood swings, and done something, anything, to have prevented the tragedy.

A close friend of mine lost his son to suicide immediately after the terrorist attack in September 2001. He, too, was devastated and numbed by his boy's death, and like so many who have experienced this type of loss, later had to deal with tremendous anger at what his son had done.

Suicide is not an individual issue. Its selfishness and desperation violate our understanding of being one body in Christ. It is a statement in action that the individual does not care about the suffering he or she is going to cause others—and that the others did not care sufficiently about the individual's pain to prevent the suicide. Because it is a final act, others have no opportunity to work toward forgiveness and reconciliation or to offer help.

◆

96

Abortion. Over the past three decades, at least in this country, abortion on demand has become a polarizing issue, widely debated by all. Often, when asked about their beliefs regarding the Supreme Court case known as *Roe v. Wade,* it becomes the political litmus test for candidates for office and justices on federal and state benches.

Abortion—the medical termination of a pregnancy—is an ancient medical procedure, but in the past was primarily done only when the mother's life was in danger. Even then it was not universally acceptable, for the doctrine of many denominations, most notably the Roman Catholic Church, taught that even if the mother's life was threatened, she could not sacrifice the life of her unborn child to save her own. Nor did ecclesiastical law allow for abortion in the case of rape or incest or when medical tests indicated the child would be born with severe mental or physical deformities. Prior to the *Roe v. Wade* decision, laws in some states were changed to permit abortion in the case of rape or incest, or for other limited reasons. But even then some hospitals, especially those under the auspices of some denominations, refused to perform the procedure.

The challenge of abortion is the moral issue of killing a child, and the uncertainty of when life begins. Does it begin at conception, at a certain point during gestation, or only when the child is born? If, as some believe, life begins at conception, then abortion and even birth control are believed to be morally unacceptable because it is the taking of a human life and a violation of this commandment. If, as some believe, life begins only when the child is born, then those who hold that view believe it is morally acceptable and not a violation of this commandment.

Regardless of which position an individual, or the nation as a whole, holds, we are united in the belief that abortion does have physical, emotional, and spiritual consequences. Many women, no matter what reason they used to justify abortion, have experienced great remorse for their decisions and actions. Even years later, the memory of the experience, the questions, and the doubts still remain vibrant in the mind of the woman. The paradox is that some women who have chosen to carry a child have also suffered greatly for doing so. Although it is far less common now than in the past, some women have died in childbirth, others have experienced postpartum depression, and as we noted previously, some have suffered such great emotional trauma that they have killed their children and taken their own lives.

There are no easy and simple answers to this complex challenge. An attempt by the state or the federal government to create a unified policy—"one size fits all"—has already proven unworkable. If anything, a legal code will only add to the burden of guilt. Nor is it likely that a unanimous agreement on the morality and justification of abortion on demand will ever be reached.

Once Jesus was asked about the intentional taking of another person's life. His response was that if we hate another person so much that we wish they were dead or we fantasize about killing them, then we are as guilty as if we had committed the act. We have allowed our rage to take control of our heart and mind. We are no longer in community with that person, and we wish to usurp God's role in deciding when a person's life should come to an end. It is a destruction of the one thing God deemed most sacred of all—life itself. Jesus makes it clear: We must work at reconciliation, forgiveness, the acceptance of someone forgiving us, and restoring right relationship.

✦

From Harmony to Havoc

THE SEVENTH COMMANDMENT

Thou shall not commit adultery.

WILSON CAME INTO MY OFFICE and collapsed in a chair, looking exhausted, even defeated, his eyes red and his face drawn. For the few minutes he said nothing, my mind was reeling with worry. Had he lost his job? Did the doctor give him bad news? Without a word he gave me a letter from a lawyer, informing him that his wife of nearly thirty years had filed for divorce.

His words came in a torrent: Gretchen had been having an affair with a married friend from the country club, and was in love. The friend was planning to leave his wife; Gretchen was divorcing Wilson. She had made up her mind, and was not interested in counseling or in attempting reconciliation. Their children were grown and on their own, and she wanted one last chance at love and happiness before it was too late.

The news ripped through their country club, the community, and our church. None of us had seen it coming. If anything, Wilson and Gretchen seemed like the perfect couple who would glide into old age together. People took sides; some with Wilson, others with Gretchen. For all of us, it was a horrible time. And we all knew it had to be far worse for the two of them and their families.

What havoc we cause.

But it was not always so. In the first creation story, in the first chapter of the Book of Genesis, we find God creating the heavens and the earth, but at first it was a chaotic place without form or light. Immediately God began to establish order in the universe, starting with a separation between light and dark, then between the waters and the dry land. God created all living things, each in its own order, and as a final act of creation, brought about human life, which God likewise intended to live in harmony among the order God had created. Harkening back to this, in the *Book of Common Prayer,* we pray that God might take control of the unruly and disorderly hearts of all men and women so that we can once again live in harmony with God's creation.

In creating all living things, God gave our world the gifts of sex, sexuality, and attraction. Yet that human sexuality can be a two-edged sword: A means of horrible violence or the sublime means by which two people are emotionally, spiritually, and physically united in a magnificent bonding.

100

Anyone who has endured the pain and suffering of adultery knows it creates complete chaos in what was once an intimate and loving relationship. In a moment trust and security are destroyed, leaving in their wake anxiety, fear, and a lasting sense of utter betrayal and often unworthiness. Likewise, anyone who has committed adultery knows that the short-term pleasure of the relationship is never worth the years of pain, remorse, and sorrow. Even when the betrayed can forgive his or her betrayer, the couple can never truly get past the damage that has been done.

Conversely, anyone who has known a lifetime of fidelity in her or his marriage, despite temptations, perhaps even despite disappointment at not having experienced a wider variety of relationships—such a person knows the sense of triumph and wholeness at having remained faithful to a partner and to this commandment. It is a commandment that is not given to us to spoil our fun and deprive us of our physical and emotional pleasure, but to restrain our instinctive behaviors so that we can experience more lasting happiness and more abundant life—personally, familially, and socially. God has graciously provided us with the standard by which we can experience abundant life.

This commandment remains important to us for a number of reasons. First, the history of almost every civilization shows that family units give a culture its framework and thus its strength and stability. Family units come in a variety of constellations, but each can provide love, mutual care and support, and stability. Where marriage and family life have been supported, civilization has advanced and progress has been made on all social issues. Where marriage is not honored and family life has not been held in the highest esteem, the quality of life deteriorates. No other form of success—whether in economics, politics, the arts and sciences—can bring the joy an individual, couple, and family know when a marriage is strong. When we experience that joy, we feel an inner strength and determination to work all the harder and be even more productive and successful. Even if material success is not accomplished, joy can be found in doing life's work and making things better for other family members. But when a marriage is in trouble, especially when the trouble is caused by infidelity, it is so overwhelming that it becomes an immense challenge to make progress, much less find happiness, in any other area of life.

◆

The successes and failures of other civilizations and cultures teach us in this regard. For example, one reason the Egyptians prospered and sustained such a long-lived and powerful empire was because they emphasized the importance of a stable family and home life. Families ate, played, worked, and stayed together, not out of a sense of obligation or duty but because their civilization realized the benefits of it for individuals and the nation.

By contrast, the ancient Romans model the consequences of sexual immorality and the worst of moral excesses. In the pre-Republic era, Romans believed that the shortening daylight hours of autumn were a sign the gods were angry with them, and that to prevent the sun from completely disappearing, sacrifices and offerings had to be made. Never was the Romans' fear more acute than during the latter part of December. Then, by the second week in January, the astronomers noticed that the days were beginning to lengthen, leaving the people to conclude that the gods had been appeased. Each year they made sacrifices and partied in celebration of their gratitude.

In time the Romans realized that the days automatically lengthened by early January even without the offerings and sacrifices to the sun gods, but they continued their celebrations. The two-week-long orgy of drinking, eating, and sexual immorality became known as Saturnalius. During this holiday period, all the old moral constraints and inhibitions were cast aside, and nothing done during the celebration was held against a person. Realizing the serious social problems this created, the Senate banned the holiday, replacing it with a concept of gravitas, or seriousness, which was more in keeping with their lifestyle during the other fifty weeks of the year. Of course, banning the celebration did not mean it was completely forgotten. For the next several hundred years, Saturnalius remained an underground celebration, during which time the republic became a mighty empire. However, during the first century, influenced by wicked and immoral emperors such as Caligula, Nero, and others, Rome once again became infamous for its decadence and immorality, which would, by the beginning of the fifth century, contribute to its collapse.

So the challenge is to keep trust, to remain true, for where spouses are friends and lovers, families can endure almost anything, and in turn, strengthen the nation. Today we find ourselves encountering new challenges to maintaining stable marriages: commuter marriages, spouses posted overseas for years at a time, caring for elderly or sick relatives, raising grandchildren, the stresses of addiction and abuse, diseases and disability, and long-term unemployment.

Sometimes those challenges and strains become too great for a person, and solace is sought outside the marriage. Yet, other couples similarly challenged find that their marriages have been strengthened by facing the problems together, faithfully. I once served as a civilian chaplain at a Canadian Forces base that hosted the Maple Flag exercises each summer. Pilots and air crews from NATO countries came to the base for training—and some off-duty partying. I recall one Friday afternoon asking a corporal about his plans for the weekend. He said he was going to stay on base because there were too many temptations in town, and added, "I'm a married man who wants to keep it that way." He understood that a short-term pleasure is not worth the long-term chaos of marital infidelity.

The second problem with adultery is the anger and fear it typically creates. Adultery spawns betrayal, suspicion, self-doubt, mistrust, and anger. When the adulterer is discovered, his or her partner feels betrayed and hurt. All hopes of a happy life together are dashed. Emotionally, the partner feels crushed because the one person in whom they had invested their hopes, dreams, and much of their life has done the thing that can most destroy a loving relationship. It is hard for any couple to withstand the questions and crisis of adultery.

And questions there are—endless, unresolved questions: Why did he or she do this to me? What did the lover do, say, or have that I don't? Why doesn't he or she find me attractive and interesting anymore? What have I done to cause this? What am I doing wrong? Why is this happening to me? Am I still loved? Am I going to be deserted and left to face life alone? Indeed, am I even worthy of being loved if my spouse could do this to me?

103

Even if forgiveness is granted, the nagging questions lurk: If a spouse is late coming home, is it because he or she has stopped to see someone else? Who was the person who called on the telephone but immediately hung up without saying anything? Is my spouse on a diet, exercising more, or wearing new clothes because he or she has someone else?

When adultery is the cause of a divorce, and the innocent spouse meets another person, all the old emotional baggage is brought into the new relationship. All the old anxieties and fears creep back into the mind, and it whirls in negativity. Even with counseling it is almost impossible to break free of the emotional damage done in a previous relationship.

When children live in an adulterous home, the problems can be passed on to the next generation. When the children are grown and ready to establish their own permanent relationship with another person, having witnessed the trauma and turmoil in their parents' relationship, they may either imitate them or be so fearful of being betrayed that they cannot open their hearts to another. They may also have residual anger toward their parents, take sides, or be emotionally distant from them.

Invariably those fears turn to anger—anger at the betrayer, anger at the betrayal, even anger at all other men or all other women. In the worst scenario, this type of anger can lead to violence, homicide, or rape. And sometimes the anger is turned inward and becomes debilitating depression that saps the vitality out of life or leads to suicide.

Third, paternity makes keeping the commandment important. A man has a vested interest in being certain that the children of his household are his own. In an era long before the development of DNA and blood tests, if a father was going to raise, care for, protect, and educate his children, if he was going to give a dowry when his daughter married or turn over his estate to his children at his death, he had economic reasons for being certain they were indeed his biological children, and this commandment hoped to reinforce behavior that guaranteed this. As a matter of pride, continuity in the family and community, stability, and freedom from shame, deception, and anxiety, a man then—and now—wants complete confidence that the children he is supporting and caring for are biologically his, and not the result of an adulterous affair.

This remains an important matter of concern today, just as in the past. Although DNA testing can establish for certain the parentage of a child, obedience to this commandment relieves parents of the horrible accusations and arguments that arise from such uncertainty and provides for family stability and harmony. Hearing of fathers shocked and angered to find out that the children they presumed to be their own are the result of their wives' affairs, or hearing, sometimes long after a father is dead, that he had a second family kept well hidden from his wife and children, reminds us of the need for faithfulness—and of the pain that ensues without it.

For whatever reason unfaithfulness occurs, the result is always the same—chaos, confusion, scandal, betrayal, and a host of other problems.

Fourth, indulging in adultery increases the likelihood of becoming infected with a sexually transmitted disease (STD); faithfulness to one's partner goes far toward preventing it. Some claim that HIV/AIDS will be as devastating to the people of the twenty-first century as was the Black Death in the Middle Ages, creating economic chaos and international instability. Others fear that it may bring about the end of all human life. As I write, the epidemic is once again growing in this country, and in some parts of Africa, over 20 percent of the population is already infected with the deadly HIV virus, for which there is currently neither a preventative vaccine nor a cure. And those are only the reported cases! Although some people are infected through blood transfusions, innocent children are born with the virus carried in their mother's bloodstream before birth, and others become infected through contaminated needles, the vast majority of new cases are the direct result of promiscuity.

105

Because the HIV/AIDS virus is so prevalent and terrifying, we forget the nearly fifty other STDs. Our rather casual approach to sex and our overreliance on prophylactics as a safeguard against the spread of STDs can result in tragedy. Even though STDs such as syphilis are typically not fatal or untreatable, the chaos they wreak on the lives of those who are infected and their partners is enormous.

It is cold comfort to know that there is nothing new about this. When the Crusaders began returning home from the Middle East in the twelfth century, STDs became rampant throughout much of Europe, and later spread through the Western Hemisphere. The cause was simple: Married foot soldiers and knights who had made vows of fidelity in their Christian marriage violated their promises; unmarried men who had been taught to wait until marriage before having sexual relations did not wait—and the result was widespread contagion.

G. Corwin Stoppel

The shame of being infected with one of these diseases, the horrifying knowledge that it was caught through an illicit relationship, and the sheer wickedness of infecting an innocent partner have devastated many homes, ruined marriages, and brought heartache and hardship to many people. When two people remain chaste before their marriage, and then remain faithful in their relationship, the danger of contracting these diseases is greatly reduced.

Fifth, this commandment was very likely a response to a Canaanite belief that during orgasm, a person encounters their deity. For that reason worshippers, typically men, would visit the temple or shrine and engage in sexual relations with a cult priestess. That may seem quite strange to our way of thinking, but in a more primitive, agrarian society, fertility—whether it was human, animal, or plant—was seen as closely connected with divine action. Part of the problem faced by the Israelites as they migrated into the Promised Land was that many of the pagan temples were little more than officially sanctioned brothels.

Throughout the Old Testament, we read that this practice is completely unacceptable to God and the people of God. Just as they were to remain pure and chaste in their worship of God, they also were to avoid sexual immorality under the guise of a false religion.

Still today the sexual-emotional bond between husband and wife is considered so sacred and so important to uphold that the Marriage Rite in the Episcopal *Book of Common Prayer* suggests that human marriage signifies to us the union between Christ and his Church. Similarly, in the New Testament epistles, Paul instructs us that the bond between Jesus and the Church can be likened to a groom's deep love for his bride.

Perhaps more than any other, this commandment against adultery provides the opportunity for us to experience instant personal happiness and true lasting joy.

Finally, when we read this commandment and the many additional Old and New Testament passages that amplify it, we realize it is very antiwoman. From the beginning women are portrayed as seductresses and tempters and even aggressors. It is Eve who gets blamed for yielding to the suggestions of the serpent, who first disobeys God and then tempts Adam to eat the forbidden fruit. Later we read the saga of Samson yielding to the temptations and seductions of Delilah. And in the tragic story of Tamar, her family implies that it is her fault that her stepbrother raped her. It almost appears as if every woman has insatiable physical appetites and is lying in wait to seduce every possible male she encounters. Statements made by Paul about the role of women remind us that much of the New Testament—and more of the Old—is out of touch with contemporary Western standards of equality between the sexes. Such attitudes seem so out of touch with today's reality that it is tempting to write off all these instructions as irrelevant. The cultural differences press us to look at the entire Bible far more critically and discern the message of God's love and care for all people.

The Church has done a tremendous disservice to itself and its constituents and potential members by portraying all women in the stark terms of either "Madonna" or "whore," with little gray area in between. Women are defined as either wholly evil or wholly good, and locked into one category or the other. We see this in how the Church has defined Mary, the mother of Jesus, as the perpetual "good girl" virgin while condemning Mary Magdalene as a whore whose redemption came only by her confession and submission to Jesus. By portraying women as one-dimensional rather than multidimensional, and by placing all the blame for male sexual impropriety on them, we have diminished the fullness of women, abdicated responsibility, and rejected the wholeness of God's creation.

The Bible was written in a patriarchal age. Women, for the most part, were classified with slaves and children as little more than property. We must recognize the roles of revelation and evolution as we progress in our faith and come to see that some aspects of the Old and New Testaments are no longer as relevant as they once were.

To look at the Old and New Testament stories in the context of contemporary society is never easy. It is far easier to resort to "that old-time religion that was good enough for

◆

107

father" than to discern, debate, and sometimes disagree with their interpretation. For those who reject the idea of postbiblical revelation or an evolution of faith and social progress, we need only look to our Lord's comments when a group challenged him about divorce. He pointed out that under the Mosaic codes, the reasons for divorce were far more lenient because the people were not yet ready to accept greater challenges. He then added that divorce, for any reason other than adultery, was against God's will.

When we turn to the Gospels, we find that Jesus has several comments about this commandment, in addition to the aforementioned reference. When he was asked about adultery, he said that if a man so much as looks at any woman other than his wife with lust and the desire to have sex with her, he is as guilty as if he has already committed adultery with her.

This shift is important and highly relevant to today's culture. First, it puts the onus on the male to control himself rather than to use Adam's blatant attempt at shifting the blame for his sin to Eve because she was the temptress. It is the man who has the responsibility to control his urges and to say no to what he already instinctively knows to be wrong. No one promised this would be an easy task, especially in an age when human sexuality is expressed in virtually every aspect of life, but it is required of all men and women, not just women. Second, it means that we have the responsibility of monitoring our behavior and attitudes. For example, men must share in the blame for the overly revealing women's fashions because we have had a part in creating a society that persistently promotes that. In short, men must share in the responsibility for maintaining the highest sexual ethical standards and building up the strength and solidarity of the home. Men must also look at their role in promoting and encouraging violence, especially sexual violence, as a means of gaining or maintaining control. For example, until recently the climate in the Air Force Academy gave male cadets the protection of the "old boy network," allowing them to assault female cadets and get away scot-free, while the women tended to be pushed to leave—and keep silent.

By contrast Jesus models a healthy and appropriate relationship with women. His respect and honor of his mother are to be expected, but even when he was in great agony on the cross, one of his primary concerns was for the future well-being of his mother. Beyond that we see Jesus changing attitudes by example. In his era and culture, men and women did not speak to any woman outside her own extended family, and then only if a third person was present. Men and women worshipped separately. But Jesus welcomed appropriate conversations with women, even when his society did not approve. He walked some forty miles out of the way to talk with the woman at the well; he spoke to the woman about to be stoned for having committed adultery, and forgave her of her sins; he healed women; and we now believe that women were among the disciples, albeit not the twelve who were closest to him and mentioned by name in the Gospels.

What a wonderful opportunity we have to time and again revisit this commandment in light of the changes brought about by science, technology, and the arts! When Moses delivered the Ten Commandments to the people, they lived in a relatively circumscribed and homogenous society where everyone knew their neighbors and their neighbors' activities. People could see where their neighbors were going and with whom they were talking, and could keep track of their obedience to the Ten Commandments. Even in larger cities, a type of informal community watch allowed everyone to keep track of the relationships between everyone else.

The first real change came with the popular use of the automobile. A little less than a century ago, it became possible to drive more than a few miles away from home and be somewhere where people could be relatively certain no one would know them. There, away from the watchful eyes of their neighbor, they could, if they so desired, do the things they dared not do at home. Not surprisingly, many church leaders warned of the automobile leading to adultery, fornication, and other sins.

Today we face a new challenge from the computer and the Internet. Just as it is possible to use these as a wonderful tool for research and communication, they can also be used to our detriment. The Internet is a wonderful way to electronically meet new people, and has sometimes been used successfully to meet a new partner. At the same time, it can be used as a tool for establishing a relationship outside of marriage. Even if the two people never meet, it raises serious questions about emotional and spiritual fidelity in a marriage. What starts out as a bit of fun can readily be interpreted as betrayal by a partner.

The Internet industry has also made it possible to easily access pornography. What many users claim is innocent exploration, just "seeing what is out there," is actually a form of emotional infidelity. It leaves a spouse or partner wondering about their own inadequacies and failure, feeling betrayed, and disconnected from their partner.

Out of chaos God created all things, and at the close of the sixth day, proclaimed them good. In that creation process, God created sex, and when we use this gift as God intended, it is indeed good—very, very good.

✦

110

✦

Nickel and Diming: Stealing Our Peace

THE EIGHTH COMMANDMENT

Thou shall not steal.

I BECAME A THIEF ONE DAY when I was ten. It was my only sortie into crime, and the memory of it remains with me. Not far from my father's store, Stoppel's Feed and Seed Company, was an Osco drugstore. They kept toys in the back; a peashooter that cost a nickel caught my attention. I had the money to buy it but decided to steal it, even though I knew it was wrong. I slipped the toy into my coat pocket and got out the door without being caught. Then, like any hardened, tough criminal, I scurried down the back alley—my preplanned escape route—to the safety of my father's store and an almost unlimited supply of peashooter ammunition. I noticed a woman was following me down the alley, and I was certain I'd been caught. In the two blocks I traveled, I could imagine the shame of being caught, the lecture from my parents, their disappointment, maybe even jail time. I kept checking over my shoulder to see if she was following me, and she was! Perhaps realizing my fear, the woman said she wasn't intentionally following me. Relieved or not, I lost all interest in the peashooter, buried it in the bottom of a trash bin, and vowed never to steal anything again.

When we were still young children, we began learning the basic rules of society. Among them were "Keep your hands to yourselves" and "Don't take something that doesn't belong to you." Although there were seldom any tangible rewards other than verbal praise for doing the right thing, we quickly learned that we would be punished if we did the wrong thing. It was in that same vein that God gave the people the eighth commandment: Thou shall not steal.

There is nothing unique to the Jews about this commandment. The somewhat older code of Hammurabi is just as specific about the illegality of theft and spells out the harsh punishments for those who are caught, tried (often by ordeal), and convicted. Other civilizations had similar legal codes; without exception none permitted the taking of another person's property. In those predemocratic societies, most often the legal codes were written to prohibit theft of the king's property, and only later were expanded to include the taking of anyone's property. That was something of a radical change: Because the king had been divinely appointed by a god, or even represented the deity on earth, to steal from the king was deemed to be stealing from the god. With the change to the legal codes to include theft from all people, the first inkling of the rights of the people was seen.

The reasons for the laws were simple and basic: Theft destroys the orderliness of society and it sometimes jeopardizes the life of the victim. When property is missing and presumed to be stolen, accusations quickly follow, suspicions are raised, and there is a desire for revenge. To steal another man's flock of animals deprives him of his livelihood and sole source of income. To steal his clothes means he has no shelter from the elements. To steal his weapons means he is defenseless against an enemy. But theft adds another burden, to society as a whole and to each individual: the burden of having to lock up, guard, or otherwise protect what one owns. And where theft does occur, the resulting anger and quest for revenge often lead to further destructive violence.

But if the rule against theft was indeed basic to all cultures, all societies, and in all ages, why was it necessary to include it in the Ten Commandments? First, God has always been vitally concerned about the well-being of God's people, wanting only the best for them. In a complete reversal of the prevailing attitudes of the world, this concern is especially extended to the poor and powerless, as shown in the story of David and the prophet Nathan (2 Samuel, chapter 12) when, following the king's seduction of Uriah's wife, Bathsheba, Nathan tells the apocryphal story of a poor man whose one pet sheep was stolen by a man who had everything. David is outraged at the harm done to one of his poorest subjects, and then mortified to comprehend that the story is about him, that he was the offender when he stole another man's wife. To steal anything is bad enough; to steal from a person who has little is far worse.

Many of us were raised on another story—that of "Honest Abe" Lincoln. For a time he and his partner ran a small store in New Salem, Illinois—and not very successfully, either. Business was slow and their few clients were perpetually short of money. One day a woman made some purchases, and only later did Lincoln realize that he had overcharged the woman a few cents. Rather than wait to give her the money when she next returned, much less just keep it, according to what may be an apocryphal story, Lincoln walked several miles to give it back to her that day.

Second, the commandment against stealing is important because how we treat material things is a reflection of our relationship with Jesus and God. Jesus said almost six times as many things about how we treat our possessions as he did about any other subject. The reasons for scrupulous honesty are simple: To steal is to create chaos and disorder in what God intended to be an orderly world, and it is a violation of another person. To steal from someone is, in effect, to steal the time and effort it took to earn that object. It is to make a person forfeit at least a small portion of her or his time on earth.

When we think of theft, we often think of it primarily in terms of material, tangible possessions, and most often that is indeed the case. We see what someone else has, and if we have decided we want it, we take it without permission or payment. Police never cease to be amazed when

◆

113

they discover that a thief has taken the most useless of junk, or has sufficient money to pay for what he attempted to steal—as I did when I stole the peashooter.

The Old Testament record speaks mainly of theft of material possessions—livestock, tools and farm implements, clothing, money, food, and anything else that could be carried away. As for stealing food, in many ancient communities throughout Israel, it was quite common for the men to dig a large, deep pit where all households could store their commodities in large clay or terra-cotta jars. Each container had the name or mark of the individual or family on it so that they could identify their own property. There, in the relatively cool air of the underground chamber, it was preserved for future use. When someone needed grain or dried fruit or meat, they could go to this community warehouse, find their own jar, and take home what they needed. However, a thief could lift the lid of someone else's jar to steal what belonged to their neighbor.

But there were and are other forms of theft besides that of material possessions. In the story of the twin brothers Jacob and Esau, we see how Jacob and his mother conspired to cheat Esau out of what should have been his rightful inheritance as the oldest son. In addition to receiving all the land and tangible property, Esau should have received his father's final blessing, which would have made him the hereditary leader of their extended family or clan upon his father's death. Instead, Jacob and his mother deceived his father so that Jacob received his brother's birthright, then profited from it—but also discovered that his theft came with a high emotional and spiritual cost.

These days the costs of an individual's theft have an effect far beyond individual families. The financial scandals among some of the nation's largest corporations, like Enron and Tyco, are but two of many examples where men and women placed in positions of trust have intentionally deceived shareholders and employees. Hard on the heels of those scandals were the after-hour manipulations in mutual funds, which also defrauded—stole money from—investors, hundreds of thousands of regular Joes and Janes who saw their financial security—typically their pension savings—snatched from them. Like false prophets of biblical times, these company yes-men flatter the executive boards, fill their pockets, and steal the company's reputation and fortunes. Over the centuries technology changes, but the human heart does not. There are many new ways to violate this commandment: identity theft, intellectual property theft, industrial espionage, the land speculation and fraud of the 1830s, the railroad stock fraud of the 1870s to 90s, the stock market fraud of the 1920s—but all are variations on the age-old theme of taking something that does not belong to one.

One particular kind of deceit is common to most of us: the theft of time. When I was growing up, the highest accolade an employee could earn for himself or herself was that of a "steady worker." It meant that he or she came to work on time or even a few minutes early, settled down to the job, and did not waste time on breaks or personal affairs. The employee didn't slip away early for an overly long lunch or leave work early. He or she did all that was expected and more, and without complaint. Such an individual, even when there were lay-offs and rising unemployment, had a far better chance of staying employed or being able to find another job because of his or her reputation. The reason is simple: A lazy worker, one who takes inordinate breaks, one who doesn't do the job so that someone else has to do it, costs his or her employer extra money. That, too, is a form of theft.

115

But we can also steal time from our family and others, and even ourselves, by spending endless hours in front of the television or computer. We are stealing the most precious gift we can give them—our time. I just caught myself doing it—taking what I told myself would be a short break from writing to check my e-mail messages. Somehow I got distracted looking up the baseball scores, checking tomorrow's weather, and then playing three games of solitaire. So much for my life of crime ending with shoplifting when I was ten years old. I just stole an hour from my wife, myself, and God.

Closely related to this is another form of theft—stealing from God. At the offertory we sometimes say or sing that all things come from God, and that we are only returning a portion of what God has given us. God's standard has always been the tithe. God's people are to return to his ser_vice one tenth of what they receive from him. This creates two dangers. The first is trying to cheat God out of what he expects. This ties in with the next commandment, about not being scrupulously honest. The other danger is in believing that scrupulous obedience to the tithe is all that God expects of us, and that we need do nothing more.

We are expected to return to God what is asked of us, the tithe. But a close reading of the Old Testament also indicates that we are invited to give beyond that—our offerings. In other words, the tithe is the minimal amount, and those who are able to do so are encouraged to give even more.

To be committed to tithing means that one is fully committed to doing the work of God. Often our parishes and denominations, as well as the parochial and more secular charitable organizations, are severely hampered because of a lack of funds. If we were not stealing from God by neglecting to give our tithe, so many more projects could be underwritten and so many more people could be helped. We would have adequate medical care, education, and a host of other basic human needs met; the division between the "haves" and the "have-nots" of the Western and third-world nations would be minimized; the level of international tension and anger would be greatly diminished.

116

We can also steal from God by not making good on our commitment of personal support and presence. Few things are more demoralizing than to worship in a nearly empty church. It is demoralizing to the cleric who has prepared for the service; it is even more demoralizing to the lay members who, after a while, begin to wonder if they are wasting their time by attending. We steal time from God by not reading our Bible on a daily basis, by not praying, by not meditating, and by not learning all we can about God's ways. For parents that is an especially important challenge, because they are meant to be an example to their children. To fulfill this aspect of the commandment requires intentional, Christ-centered living.

Such Christ-centered living calls us not to grab for ourselves more wealth, natural resources, or other limited
commodities than we need or can use. Any misuse or over-
use of resources means we are taking them from others
today or from future generations. Groups such as the
Audubon Society, the Nature Conservancy, and the Sierra
Club have championed the cause of our prudent use of
resources for the benefit of others.

Similarly, our insistence on the lowest possible price for
our purchases and, at the same time, the highest possible
return on our money means that jobs once held by workers
in this country now go to foreign countries. Just today the
local papers carried the news that another eight hundred
jobs would be lost in nearby Holland, Michigan. Claiming
the challenges of competition, Johnson Control will be out-
sourcing work to Mexico, where labor costs are one-fifth
what they are here. It's not just eight hundred employees
who will be out of work, but eight hundred families whose
futures are in jeopardy. In turn, other businesses will be
hurt, as will the churches, civic organizations, and charities
supported by those displaced employees. And all because
shareholders are demanding ever-higher returns on their
investments.

Likewise, to save a few pennies or dollars, many con-
sumers unthinkingly patronize some of the larger depart-
ment and discount stores, never realizing that their
employees are, for the most part, hired only on a part-time
basis so that the company does not have to pay benefits.
Because discount businesses are able to offer better prices,
they can drive their independently owned competitors out
of business and dominate the local economy in both the
selling of goods and the hiring of employees.

Pure and simple, this is theft. It is a matter of the wealthy
demanding to become even wealthier, often by stealing
opportunities from the poor.

When we look at this commandment in light of the
teachings of Jesus, we quickly realize how it fits with the
Second Great Commandment of loving our neighbor as

G. Corwin Stoppel

117

ourselves. Out of love and respect for our brothers and sisters, whether they are in our own household or half a world away, we are responsible for treating all others honestly and with love. We are also responsible for using our assets and resources in such a way that we do them no harm, but rather build them up. We can look at this as an onerous task or as someone else's responsibility, or we can delight in the fact that God has entrusted this work to us. As the Body of Christ, we can explore and find creative ways of achieving true economic justice.

118

✦

Honest to God

THE NINTH COMMANDMENT

Thou shall not bear false witness against thy neighbor.

L ATE ONE NIGHT MY LITTLE DOG woke me up, barking at something outside. I assumed it was an animal either in my garden or in the cemetery between the rectory and the church. To my horror I saw a couple of young men kicking over tombstones, and quickly called the police. Within minutes the Mounties had them in custody. The next morning I was called to the court to give my testimony. On my way to the witness stand, I was intercepted by the bailiff: "Raise your right hand and put your left hand on the Bible. Do you promise to tell the truth, the whole truth, and nothing but the truth, so help you, God?" to which I was expected to say, "I do." It was straight out of *Perry Mason* and *Law and Order*—the very heart of our judicial system.

In or out of court, whether we make a formal statement or not, a credible witness and a reputation for honesty are highly valued. Indeed, we will generously forgive the mistakes others make, but we are slow to forgive and trust the deceptive person. We have forgiven everyone from elementary-age children to presidents for their blunders, but once they are caught in an intentional lie, we are wary of everything they tell us in the future. It is hard enough to earn a reputation for being honest; it is all the harder to re-earn it.

Even though this commandment, like several others, is

phrased in the negative, the positive implications are clear: We are always to tell the truth. More than that, we are to tell the whole truth, not just a part of it—perhaps the part that we think others want to hear or the part we want to tell others for our own comfort or advantage. Anything less than complete honesty is ultimately destructive.

Both the Old and New Testaments make it clear that God abhors anything less than the truth. Sprinkled throughout the Old Testament are verses and stories that make it obvious that to knowingly speak (and by implication, write) an untruth is wrong. As noted in the sixth commandment, when the elders or judges met to hear the evidence against someone accused of murder or another serious crimes, they relied solely on the statements made by eyewitnesses. Because this was in an age long before forensic science and because the laws made no provision for circumstantial evidence, the true testimony of witnesses was critical for justice to be served. In the case of the most serious crimes, at least two credible eyewitnesses were required before a trial could be held. Each witness was independently examined. Their evidence could not be contradictory, but neither could it appear to have been prepared in collaboration or with coaching and instruction from a third person. Further, the witnesses had to be men of good repute, of age, and completely disinterested in the verdict. (In that patriarchal age, the testimony of women and children was not permitted as they were not deemed credible witnesses.)

Thus, in the trial of Jesus before the Temple authorities, we see the difficulty his prosecutors had in convicting him. They could not find two eyewitnesses who fit the criteria to give a legitimate testimony. The chief priest, Caiaphas, called in several witnesses, but either their stories did not match or it was obvious they had been in collusion, much to his frustration. Even Pilate became so frustrated by this perversion of justice that he symbolically washed his hands of the matter—and yet allowed the crucifixion, if only to silence the demands of the crowd.

Far less serious were business agreements between two individuals. It was an era when written documents were uncommon and eyewitness testimony was relied on. Once

the witnesses were present, the two individuals would publicly agree to their transaction, knowing that if a dispute
ever needed to be adjudicated, the witnesses could be
called to give testimony about what they had seen and
heard. Today we follow in that same tradition when we sign
important legal documents that require one or more witnesses and a notary public to affix a formal seal.

The attention to detail in the amplification and extra-
canonical instructions of the Old Testament—the Talmud
and the Midrash—on the role of witnesses demonstrates
the solemnity the Israelites attached to scrupulous judicial
and civil honesty. Those laws mandate that a false witness
must pay the same penalty as the accused. Thus, if a witness knowingly gave false testimony in a capital offense, he
was required to forfeit his own life; if the penalty was the
loss of an eye or a limb, forfeiture of money, or any other
penalty, the false witness was required to suffer that same
penalty. Those regulations served as a preventative measure against giving false testimony and emphasized the
importance of telling the truth.

Although the Old Testament primarily emphasized the
importance of spoken honesty, by direct implication, that
principle was extended to the written word. This became
increasingly important as the Israelite civilization became
more established, as domestic and international trade
increased, and when real estate and personal property
became more important. Surprisingly, found among the
cache of documents known as the Dead Sea Scrolls were
some bills of sale for real estate, and by this time—the first
century BCE—the realtor was a woman. The culture had
already changed, allowing women to give testimony in civil
matters.

121

It is one thing to make an accidental mistake when
speaking or writing. If I mistakenly tell my wife that I am
going to the drugstore when I meant to say I was going
to the hardware store, that is a mistake. There was no
intention to deceive her. I might have been distracted, a little muddled in my thinking, or had a mental hiccup
between my brain and my mouth. Mistakes like that are

understandable because they happen to us all. Or, if I make an error adding up numbers, it could be a legitimate mistake. But if I tell Pat I am going to one place when I have already decided to go somewhere else, or if I start doing some intentionally creative accounting, that is quite another matter. That is when the line is crossed from making an honest mistake to telling a lie.

Discerning between honest mistakes and intentional falsehoods is important. As much as we want honesty and accuracy of information, we don't always get it. Part of the grace and maturity we develop in our lives is the ability to give others—and ourselves—the freedom to be truly human. However, the time typically comes when we realize that another person is not giving us accurate information. Perhaps it is because of exhaustion, a mental or physical problem, or sheer carelessness—it doesn't matter; we need to verify what that person is telling us.

And then there are the times when we know we are dealing with a habitual liar. As Hitler demonstrated, the "big lie," when told loud enough and often enough, is far more effective than many small ones. Unfortunately, a great many people and institutions chose to take their text from Hitler rather than the Scriptures.

Some current examples come quickly to mind: President Nixon announcing that he was not a crook and had nothing to do with the break-in at the Watergate Hotel; President Clinton assuring us that he never had sexual relations with a White House intern; President Bush and leading administration officials insisting on the presence of weapons of mass destruction in Iraq; and the financial lies from Enron, Tyco, and other corporations. Usually only individuals or large corporations with great power can successfully tell the big lie.

Why does the lie work? Because those with power and authority tell us what we want to hear. Hitler succeeded because of the economic chaos and social unrest in post–World War I Germany; U.S. presidents succeed in telling the big lie because we want to believe that our highest elected official is not a criminal or an adulterer, or that he has information that is not available to the rest of us.

Corporations succeed with the big lie because we want to believe that their accountants are honest and our investments are safe—their success instills a sense of trust. Users of the big lie are masters of psychology; they understand how to appeal to the masses and they are in important places, so that we want to believe them.

When the big lie is told, chaos results. Germany had long been a nation of high achievement in the arts and sciences, but once the people believed the big lie, they became guards in concentration camps. President Nixon was impeached; President Clinton was so distracted by the impeachment proceedings and so weakened that our national defenses suffered; President Bush's big lie led to a war with Iraq and the deaths of countless Iraqi civilians and hundreds of American service personnel; the big lies from Wall Street sent the Dow Jones Averages plummeting, ruined the American economy, and destroyed the personal savings of hundreds of thousands of innocent investors. What is worse, it has damaged the credibility of all politicians and most financial advisors. We are wary of them now and slow to trust anything any of them say.

◆

Most of us will never be in a position to successfully tell the big lie. However, we are not without our own opportunities to break this commandment. Our cache of methods includes lying to others, lying to ourselves, and lying to God. Let's look at each of them.

We lie to others. Police officers have come to expect errant motorists to lie. Drunk drivers try to convince the officer who pulled them over that they had only one or two beers; speeders say they didn't see the sign or were on their way to the hospital. We tell our creditors that the check is in the mail, our wives that we'll be home right after work, our children that we'll take them to the beach on Saturday.

We do it because we want to protect ourselves from hurt or from paying the penalty for our mistake. We want to avoid the shame, repercussions, or confrontation that may come from speaking the truth. We want to get out of trouble or, conversely, get someone else into trouble.

G. Corwin Stoppel

Sometimes we do it to draw attention to ourselves. Somewhere in my office is my father's plaque, which reads, "Lord, someday let me catch a fish so large that even I do not have to stretch the truth." Well, the sad fact is that few of us do catch that trophy, get a hole in one on the golf course, or knock the game-winning ball over the fence. In fact, we live such ordinary lives that we feel we need to embellish the truth—just a little, of course—to add some stature to our life or to strengthen our reputation.

Telling campfire stories about the "big one that got away" or regaling buddies about past triumphs is one thing. Such storytelling has long been a traditional form of bonding with friends. The real difficulty comes when we begin to lie about our achievements, background, and education in an attempt to deceive another person or organization. One of the most common ways this happens is by "padding" a resume. People may grossly exaggerate their work or educational record in the hope of securing a better job or getting a promotion. They might claim an educational degree they did not earn from a school they never attended. They might claim to be licensed or certified. It is little wonder that employment agencies and human resource directors do careful background checks to make sure the information they are given is accurate. Conversely, people lie when they intentionally neglect to list times of unemployment, or even worse, an arrest and conviction for a past crime. Such intentional deceptions are usually grounds for immediate termination of employment.

We lie to ourselves. Most of us graze a little too heartily at holidays or throughout the years, and we brush off the reality by saying that we're a "tad heavy," when the truth of the matter is we are just plain too fat. Sometimes we lie to ourselves through denial: The little twinge we feel in our chest really isn't anything, or the lump we feel is certainly benign and nothing to worry about. We can be in this state of denial about our finances, our relationships, or virtually anything else.

The difficulty is that we end up staying stuck. As long as we are convinced that everything is all right, that there is nothing we need to do, then we will never work on the problem. So, the overweight person becomes morbidly obese, the cancerous tumor metastasizes, or we file for personal bankruptcy. Instead of being honest with ourselves and addressing the issue, we let it get worse, to the point of no return. Often it is because we want to believe that our present life is only a dress rehearsal for the next, and that we have more time to do the work we need to do—yet we know better than that.

The other problem with lying to ourselves is that after a while, we begin to believe our own lies. The fellow who warmed the bench on the high school football team has told himself—and others—that he was a star letterman so many times that eventually he begins to believe his own story. The individual who claims she is descended from some long-extinct line of European royalty begins to believe that she truly is, and that any day she will be invited back home to assume the throne.

The old tale of the emperor's new clothes tells of an emperor who is determined to have the finest outfit the world has ever seen, and his tailors were petrified of disappointing him. In a moment of sheer brilliance, they do nothing, but they lie to the emperor and tell him that only a truly distinguished ruler will be able to see the outfit. He takes off his old robes, believes he is putting on a new garment, and stands naked in front of the mirror, actually believing he is wearing something. It is only when he walks down the street stark naked, believing he is clothed, that he is brought back to reality when a young boy tells the truth: The emperor is naked.

The final, major way we can lie is to lie to God. We are first introduced to this concept in the Bible, in the story of Adam and Eve in the Garden of Eden after they have eaten the forbidden fruit. We are told that their eyes were opened and they became aware of their nakedness and were ashamed. They tried hiding from God, and when God catches up with them, Adam and Eve compound their problem by lying to God. Adam told God that Eve gave him the forbidden fruit; Eve told God that it was the serpent's fault. Lying to God is not one of humanity's brightest moments because it never works. Not that we don't try!

From my studies and personal experiences, I think we try lying to God because we don't want to anger him. My first wife, Lori, died suddenly and unexpectedly of a massive aneurysm in her brain stem early one morning in late July 1996. She was gone before she collapsed to the floor. I was absolutely devastated, but fortunately had wonderful support from her family and mine, as well as the members of All Saints' Church here in Saugatuck. After the initial shock and grief and after family members went home, I returned to work about two weeks later. I was convinced that working and getting back into a routine would be the best thing for me, and maybe it was, even though my heart wasn't always in it. I kept going through the motions of being a good parish priest, but something was wrong.

It wasn't until I told God in no uncertain words that I was furious with him because of all that had happened, all the dreams that were cut short, and now being alone, that I started to spiritually, emotionally, and physically heal. And the reason I didn't initially tell God I was so angry is that I didn't want to upset him. Of course, God knew everything that was in my heart before I even said it, but I wasn't being honest with him—and that meant he wasn't able to do much to help me heal. After I let God have it good and hard, I was able to move on. And God didn't angrily punish me because of my honesty. God is big enough to handle even our honest fury.

In the popular television series *The West Wing,* one of the characters is killed in a senseless automobile accident. After the funeral President Bartlett told the Secret Service agents to close the doors because he wanted to be alone. Even as the doors were being shut, the president launched into a burst of anger at God—in Latin, I might add. It was a natural human response to his bitterness. Within hours of the program's screening, an outburst of indignation came from many Christians, who believed that the president had committed a terrible offense by daring to express his honest emotions to God.

126

I am convinced that if we are going to live out this commandment and live healthy spiritual lives, we need to be honest with God. And that includes being honest about our doubts and skepticism about many of the things we read in the Bible. Sometimes I almost envy strict, hard-core fundamentalists who are convinced that everything they read in the Old and New Testaments should be taken exactly at face value. They don't have to wrestle with some of the tough challenges that begin with Genesis and end with Revelation. They don't have to debate, disagree, or do anything other than point to a verse or passage and then leave it at that. It would certainly make my life simple if I didn't have to do anything more than that!

Like many others, to make that claim would not be honest—with myself, with the members of my parish, and with God. I have questions about nearly everything I read in the Old and New Testaments. I have some real questions as to whether the Creation story in Genesis happened exactly as it is written or if it is a poetic description of God's actions. Were the Israelites really in the wilderness for exactly forty years, or does it mean they were there for as long as it took to shake the Egyptian religion out of their system and come to understand the nature of God? I've got a long list of questions about Jesus, starting with the virgin birth through the miracles and on to the post-Resurrection stories of having a fish breakfast with the disciples. I have another long list of questions under the heading "heaven."

127

Staunch fundamentalists have it lucky—they have all the answers immediately given to them: It's in the Bible. For that matter, at the other end of the spectrum, Deists are just as fortunate because they deny anything and everything that doesn't make sense to them. Like many others I'm somewhere in between. I have a lot of unanswered questions and a number of doubts. I'll have them until I find answers.

I don't think that having questions and doubts means I am lacking in faith because I don't believe God asks us to leave our brains at the door when we come to church or when we study our Bibles. Like a good number of saints, our refrain becomes: "I believe. Help me in my unbelief."

G. Corwin Stoppel

Spiritual growth and knowledge of the whole holy truth come only when we are truthful in admitting to God that we need some help in understanding and believing as we make our spiritual safaris.

✦

✦

A Peaceful Heart

THE TENTH COMMANDMENT

Thou shall not covet.

ENVY SOMETIMES CATCHES us by surprise. My worst birthday was my twenty-fifth, and I swear that it had nothing to do with taking the youth group on a camping trip to what I am sure was Mosquitoville, Minnesota, nor that Elvis had died a day or so earlier. Never mind that I didn't care for his music. I set out to intentionally make it my worst birthday because I was bitterly jealous of the sum-total achievements of my classmates from both Morningside College, where I did my undergraduate work, and Duke Divinity School. I was twenty-five years old and not yet a multimillionaire, a bishop, a champion athlete, the owner of a Rolls Royce, an award-winning published author, nor an acclaimed denizen of the lecture circuit— nor had I been elected to any political office greater than the Sargeant, Minnesota, village council. At least one of my classmates had accomplished one or more of those things, but I was mad at the world and myself because I had not done all of them. As far as I was concerned, life was unfair and miserable, and I was being singled out and personally short-changed. Not only was I miserable, but when my parents suggested a party to celebrate my twenty-fifth year, I told them I didn't want it. Now that I think of it, they deserved the party for putting up with me for a quarter century! That's the problem when we yield to the temptations of violating this commandment. We are filled with bitterness, misery, and anger.

But here I am, a quarter of a century and a few odd years later, and I am not a bishop (thank God!), still no athlete, driving an elderly midsized car, still not elected to office (again, thank God), and the author of one book that is so far away from the *New York Times* Best-Seller List that it is laughable. And I am having the time of my life. We all had a good laugh recently when a member of the vestry handed me a prepaid membership in the American Association of Retired Persons. Life is good. Life is fun. And I believe the one important reason is that I am working on fulfilling this tenth commandment. I wish everyone could share in that joy, but not all my friends have caught on to it yet.

Maybe it is because I am having so much fun that I am sensitive to those who have not yet discovered the true joy of obeying this commandment. A few years ago, several of us went for a walk along the boardwalk here in Saugatuck, delighting in the sight of the boats in the harbor. But one member of our group wasn't enjoying a single moment, and was constantly fussing that he couldn't afford a boat. After a little while, someone told him: "Look, X, even if you could afford a boat, you'd be miserable because it wasn't the biggest one in the harbor. And even if you had the largest boat here, you'd still be worried that somewhere someone might have a bigger one. You'll never be satisfied."

That will long be my best definition and explanation of coveting what someone else possesses. That one brief moment, at least for me, made this commandment come alive.

130

This commandment is radically different from the other nine. Whereas the first four commandments instruct us in our relationship with God, and the next four instruct us in how to interact with other people and things so that there can be peace and harmony in our corporate life, this tenth commandment is internal. This commandment instructs us on how we should think and feel. Others can observe whether or not we worship only God, maintain the holiness of God's name (at least when they are with us), honor our parents, and protect the sanctity of life, property, and marriage, but no one can see our hearts and minds. It is only when we act on our feelings and thoughts that disobedience to the tenth commandment has more than personal consequences.

The challenge of this commandment is that if we violate it and yield to the temptations of jealousy and envy, it can have a detrimental effect on virtually every other aspect of our lives. Whenever we give in to temptations, it means that our ego has instantly taken charge of our life, and that everything else, including God, is squeezed out. We allow ourselves to become absolutely obsessed and possessed by our lust for an object—an artificial or man-made thing—or for the recognition of others. Instantly we find ourselves serving our desires and passions rather than the Lord God.

To a great extent, the constant violation of this commandment has created most of the problems in our world, and we see it happening on almost all levels. On an international level, we have seen one country invade another for its natural resources, to create an empire, to build up its market or gain less expensive access to other resources, or to enslave its people. For example, at the end of the nineteenth century, when many European nations were creating large empires, the United States felt that it was falling behind. To that end we annexed Hawaii, went to war with Spain to acquire the Philippines, Cuba, and Puerto Rico, and then engineered a coup in Panama against the Colombians so that we could build our canal. We built our canal, but at the expense of destabilizing Latin America and creating no end of international tensions for ourselves and others.

131

Other examples quickly come to mind, such as in Israel between the Israeli government and the Palestinians. Palestinians are considered second-class citizens in their own country, often badly mistreated by the government, and the situation remains so serious that there is constant bloodshed. Many ethnic Palestinian Christians have fled the country because of the abuse they have received from the two major factions.

On a national level, as the news media and our own experiences make us keenly aware, in many places there is a wide disparity between affluence and poverty. We are all aware of the plight of our inner-city neighborhoods and ghettos. Those who do not have the things they see others possessing can quickly become jealous, leading to class or economic warfare that is expressed in everything from angry accusations to outbreaks of violence. Progressive nations attempt to create some sort of balance between the two groups, emphasizing the important role of a broad middle class, knowing that too much wealth in the hands of a few and too much poverty experienced by many will ultimately lead to disaster.

However, it is on the local, individual level where we become most aware of the significance of the tenth commandment. Nearly all of us, to a greater or lesser degree, are envious and jealous of others. I could envy someone with a bigger house and a bigger garage to store their fleet of automobiles and other "big-boy toys," such as boats. I can easily envy someone who can afford to belong to an expensive or more prestigious country club, who owns a more expensive automobile or wristwatch, who has better clothes and finer accessories or some other tangible item.

Our envy isn't limited to tangible things. We can look enviously at someone else's son or daughter who has seemingly achieved more than our own has, or at the man or woman who seemingly has more grace, style, athletic skill, talent, popularity, or physical beauty than we do. Sometimes we turn on our spouse or other family members and, even though we may not come out and say that we are jealous of others, rail at them for not living up to an ideal of perfection that we see in someone else. We express it in our frustration: Why don't we have a newer car, go on better and longer vacations, have a bigger house in a better neighborhood? Behind those accusatory questions is the real issue: Why aren't we more successful like our neighbor, our brother, or someone else, so that we can have all the things their family enjoys?

The American poet Edwin Arlington Robinson (1869–1935) describes precisely that sort of situation and its sometimes tragic consequences in his short poem "Richard Cory." The neighbors are baffled when he commits suicide, thinking that because he has so many material things, he must be incredibly happy and enjoying the perfect life.

Whenever Richard Cory went down town
We people on the pavement looked at him;
He was a gentleman from sole to crown,
Clean favored, and imperially slim
And he was always quietly arrayed
And he was always human when he talked
But still he fluttered pulses when he said,
"Good-morning," and he glittered when he walked.
And he was rich—yes richer than a king—
And admirably schooled in every grace
In fine, we thought that he was everything
To make us wish that we were in his place
So on we worked, and waited for the light
And went without the meat, and cursed the bread.
And Richard Cory, one calm summer night
Went home and put a bullet in his head.

133

The result of violating this commandment is tension, anger, and animosity in our homes. We can decide that we are envious of what our neighbor has, and want it for ourselves—now. Banks and other financial institutions will take advantage of our jealousy and make it possible for us to borrow great sums of money on our credit cards or through second mortgages on our homes so that we can have today what we feel we deserve, rather than saving to purchase it later. Then, when we are deeply in debt, those same institutions are quite willing to offer other refinancing packages, a debt-consolidation loan, or some other method of lending us even more money.

It is not surprising that many families have a great number of things, but also carry a huge debt load, and live in constant fear that any down turn in the economy, a serious illness, or temporary unemployment will force them into

G. Corwin Stoppel

bankruptcy. We have also been told by economists that, on the whole, we save less than 2 percent of our post-tax income, meaning we are unprepared for either emergencies or retirement.

The quest for having more things has had a tremendous impact on our consumer economy. We all seem to want more things, but we want them as inexpensively as possible so that we can have more of them. This has created a rather amusing though somewhat pathetic side to our consumerism: knockoffs. Because not everyone can afford or wishes to spend a small fortune on a Rolex watch, Versace accessories, or other luxury items, illegal imitations proliferate the market. Thus, instead of spending ten thousand dollars or more for a Rolex, the jealous or envious individual can buy a knockoff for a few dollars. Of course, it might be accurate only twice a day, and anyone with knowledge of the genuine article can quickly see that it is a cheap imitation. The same principle applies to countless other products. The fact that they are often illegal and sometimes potentially harmful is bad enough; the fact that the market for these things flourishes, due to the dark emotions of envy and jealousy, is far worse.

I believe it is a spiritual problem, because this mentality is saying we need things, even counterfeit things, to give justification to our lives; we need the appearance of status or luxury items to demonstrate our worth or value to ourselves and others. Ultimately, we are saying that the created thing is more important to us than having an upright relationship with the Creator.

But it is not only tangible things that we envy. We can be envious of almost anything in our world—from the physical appearance to the lifestyles of others. It often leads us to feeling that we are on the outside looking in, that we have been excluded. We often neglect to realize that the successful man or woman spends long hours hard at work honing their skills, and has made other sacrifices. Rather than joining them in their strenuous efforts and self-discipline, it is far easier to be envious and full of jealous complaints, often couched in the terms "It isn't fair."

In short, it seems as if almost everyone is a little envious or jealous of someone else, of being somewhere else, of doing something else. There is no limit to it. Each of us has our own list of things that spark this negative emotion in our soul, yet all of them lead directly to a restless spirit and an unquiet heart, which in turn lead to constant chaos and turmoil. The question is not whether envy and jealousy exist, but how to live and resolve this spiritual challenge so that we can keep this commandment and live the way God desires.

I do not believe that, short of a divine miracle, it is ever truly possible for anyone, except a perfect saint, to completely purge themselves of the very human emotions of envy and jealousy. We should begin by accepting the simple but harsh fact that of all the commandments, this is going to be the most difficult for us to keep because it is an internal one that deals with our heart and mind rather than with an outward behavior or action. That means we must explore how we can turn it into something positive, beneficial, and practical. The first step is to stop denying the existence of our envy and jealousy.

✦

A good place to begin is to follow the ancient dictum of the great Greek philosopher Socrates, who taught, "Know thyself." Our task is to be able to identify and specifically name those things that make us envious. For one person it might be a neighbor's house; for another it may be someone's wealth, vacation experiences, education, physique, or any other conceivable tangible or intangible attribute. Only when we specifically name it can we move forward.

The next step is to determine if we can do something to change our negative emotions into positive ones. If I am envious of my neighbor's new car, I have several options. I can stay envious and resent him for what he owns, but that will only create an ever-widening rift between us. A better choice would be to appreciate the success my neighbor has enjoyed and to share in his excitement about his new car. Even if I can never afford an automobile like his, I can appreciate the style, features, and comfort. There is a wide gulf between appreciation and admiration and the negative and forbidden emotion of envy. It takes maturity, wisdom, and discernment to know the difference and live in the positive.

That same principle can be applied to almost any other aspect of life. If we see something we admire and believe to be right and good, instead of being envious, we can try to earn it for ourselves. It can be anything from "the vacation of a lifetime" that comes after years of saving to a healthy body and lifestyle.

Through discernment we begin to realize that some things are beyond our powers, no matter how hard we might work. So, even though the potential is always there for every parish priest, I know I am never going to be elected a diocesan bishop, much less Archbishop of Canterbury. As an adjunct professor at a small university, I know I am not likely to be given the opportunity for tenure. As a writer for Cowley Publications, I am not likely to be a threat to Jan Karon (the Mitford series) or J. K. Rowling (the Harry Potter books) on the *New York Times* Best-Seller List. I can work as hard as I might, but some things just aren't going to happen. And that leaves me with a choice: I can become bitterly jealous and envious of those who have enjoyed greater success, or I can enjoy my own accomplishments. I have chosen the second. I love serving at All Saints' in Saugatuck; I enjoy teaching my one or two classes a year (and am happy to avoid the campus politics endured by full-time faculty!); I'm grateful that Cowley wants me as one of their writers. It is sufficient. I strive to do all these things well. And therein I find my happiness.

136

Jesus himself shows us how to turn envy into trust. On one occasion the disciples were discussing material things, and there seemed to be some frustration that they weren't getting enough of the good things in life. In the Beatitudes Jesus reminds the crowd that we should not be envious of those who have enough to eat now, for the time will come when they are hungry; and that those who have much now will soon be empty. Jesus reminds them that God is aware of our needs and answers them; that God knows when a sparrow falls from the sky, the number of hairs on our heads, and that the lilies of the field are arrayed more beautifully than even King Solomon in all his splendor. Don't worry about things, and don't be envious of those who seem to have more, Jesus tells his disciples. Instead, be satisfied with what you have, and be confident that God will provide for your needs.

Finally, we come to realize that because keeping the tenth commandment can be so difficult, it is first and foremost a spiritual challenge. We can choose to live with our envy and jealousy, slowly growing in our rage, anger, and frustration at the rest of the world, at our neighbors, and even at those we do not know. Or, we can ask God, with confidence, to provide us with the strength we need to move forward and to liberate us from our negative feelings. It is a process that does not come instantly, but leads us to beginning to be the men and women God wants us to be.

◆

G. Corwin Stoppel

Keeping It Simple

THE TWO GREAT COMMANDMENTS

LONG BEFORE THE STAR OF DAVID became the symbol of Israel and Judah, there was the six-petaled flower of the pomegranate, which, in the sixteenth and seventeenth centuries, was gradually converted into a star. The reason for choosing the pomegranate was simple yet significant. There are 613 seeds in the fruit. There are also 613 Misvotes, or rules for daily living (i.e., laws), that Jewish scholars identified in the Ten Commandments. Every Jewish boy memorized those laws, and at the end of the day was expected to measure his words and actions against the Misvotes. Rocking back and forth on his feet, murmuring softly to himself, he would recite the laws, much as we might examine ourselves in prayer at the end of the day. If he had kept only a few of the laws, he knew he was in dire straits with God and needed to amend his life and repent of his sins. If he had kept most of the laws, then he knew he had more work to do. If he had kept all the laws, then he could stand righteously before God.

It is little wonder, then, that someone would ask Jesus which of the commandments was the greatest. If they were expecting Jesus to give an easy and quick answer, they were soon disappointed.

Jesus said that there were just two commandments to keep—to love God with one's entire ability and to love one's neighbor as oneself. At first glance it might have seemed that Jesus had given the questioner an easy out—if you cannot keep all ten, then keep these two. However, when we recall that the Ten Commandments are divided into two sections, the first instructing us on our love, devotion, and service to the Lord God, the second focusing on our proper relationship with other people, we see that with these two commandments, Jesus is giving a summary of the two separate but related sections of the law.

Perhaps the questioner felt he had been tricked by such an answer, or that Jesus was having a little sport at his expense. That was far from the case, for in summarizing the law into two commandments, Jesus was inviting us to look at it from an entirely different perspective. Rather than being confined to a specific number of rules and regulations or always worried that another rule needs to be spelled out for us, we see that keeping the commandments is turned back to us with this simple instruction: Find your own way to do the right thing before God and your neighbor.

It is incredibly easy for us to complicate life with too many laws, rules, and regulations. For example, when the federal and state governments began collecting income taxes, the original laws were very simple. Anyone making more than X number of dollars per year was required to contribute a specified portion of their income to the public coffers. Today, less than a century later, the Internal Revenue Service codes are voluminous and so complicated that even a highly competent attorney or Certified Public Accountant has trouble comprehending all the schedules, forms, deductions, exemptions, and regulations. Even the IRS admits that it is not always able to give us clear instructions and information.

Although the law looks simple, its implications and ramifications are complicated. To make them even more complicated, society and technology are forever changing, and anyone wishing to comply with these laws is forced to reexamine them. The early Jewish rabbis, theologians, and scholars debated the law, and many of their arguments were recorded in a multivolume commentary called the Talmud. Then the Talmud was subjected to endless arguments and discussions, many of which are recorded in the even larger multivolume commentary on the commentary called the Midrash.

Thus, when Jesus condenses all the hundreds of laws into these two, he is simplifying something that had become so convoluted that it was counterproductive. He cut to the chase: Love God with all your might, look after your neighbor, and do what is right by both of them. It was each person's responsibility to discern the right thing.

A good example of something simple becoming convoluted is the matter of washing one's hands properly before a meal, which the Pharisees complained Jesus didn't do properly. First-century Israelites were not primarily concerned with personal hygiene in this rule, but with showing respect to God's provision of food by coming to the table to eat the holy gift with clean hands. But then the Pharisees devised a ritualistic way that hands had to be washed. Suddenly it was not what was in the diner's heart that mattered, it was not his or her gratitude, it was not the recognition that food came from God. What mattered was whether or not that person followed the rite of hand washing in the proper way. Some of the Pharisees were so concerned about the rite that they all but forgot about God. And that is where they and Jesus parted company.

141

Jesus teaches it is what is inside one's heart that matters. If obedience to the rite is more important, if feeling smugly superior to those who do not wash their hands the right way is what is important, then one has lost sight of God and the gift of food. If those things preoccupy your attention, you have squeezed out God, you have made your ritual an idol, and you demonstrate absolutely no love and charity for people who are different from you.

The onus for keeping the Ten Commandments or the Two Great Commandments is on each individual. We are liberated from long laws, meaningless rituals, and a sense of being either inferior or superior people. At the same time, we are to give careful thought, based on prayer, meditation, reflection, and discernment, to everything we do. As we initiate any project, as we open our mouths to speak, we must weigh our actions and words against the Two Great Commandments, asking ourselves: Does this bring glory to God? Is this something that will benefit the other person? So we seek to do the right thing; and that, according to God, is all that is required of us.